世界のナマズ

THE WORLD OF CATFISHES

by Midori Kobayagawa
Edited by Dr. Warren E. Burgesss

TS-161

*Pangasianodon gigas,*lives in the Mekong River and may reach 3 meters in length.

WRITTEN AND PHOTOGRAPHED BY:

MIDORI KOBAYAKAWA
MINORU MATSUZAKA
ARATA KAWAMOTO
MASASHI IMAI
RYU UCHIYAMA
TSUTOMU IKEDA

FUMITOSHI MORI
MINORU MATSUZAKA
NOBUHIKO AKIYAMA
MASASHI IMAI
NAOTO TOMIZAWA
DOSHIN KOBAYASHI

Originally published in Japanese under the title CATFISHES OF THE WORLD by Marine Planning Co., Tokyo, Japan.
Japanese original edition copyright 1989.
TFH claims copyright for the English translation, 1991.

PUBLISHED, PRINTED AND BOUND BY TFH PUBLICATIONS, INC., P.O.BOX 427, NEPTUNE, N.J. 07753 USA.

CONTENTS

AFRICA

Although African catfishes are not as diverse taxonomically as those of the Amazon, they include unique groups such as the Mochokidae, in which there are more than 100 species, and the Malapteruridae, which can generate electricity. African catfishes are primarily found in the three great river systems—Nile, Niger, and Zaire—as well as in some of the lakes in the eastern part of the continent. Mochokid catfishes are related to the bagrid catfishes (Bagridae), which may be found both in Africa and Eurasia. From this fact we can speculate that both continents were closely related faunally a long time ago.

The walking catfishes (Clariidae) symbolize the African continent by surviving the great differences between the dry and rainy seasons. Having specially developed air-breathing organs, they can survive in a dried swamp for long periods of time until the rains return. They can also move across wet places to better habitats by "walking." You can say that at least some African catfishes are making a desperate effort to survive.

Mochokiella paynei

Hemisynodontis membranaceus

Brachysynodontis batensoda

Microsynodontis batesii

Synodontis angelicus

Synodontis angelicus

Synodontis angelicus

Synodontis
flavitaeniatus

Synodontis
nigriventris

Synodontis
contractus

6

Synodontis pleurops

A variety of *Synodontis pleurops.*

Synodontis notatus notatus

Synodontis notatus ocellatus

Synodontis decorus

Synodontis ornatipinnis

Synodontis congicus

Synodontis nummifer

Synodontis brichardi

A variety of *Synodontis brichardi.*

Synodontis camelopardalis

Synodontis camelopardalis

Synodontis caudalis

Possibly *Synodontis caudalis.*

Synodontis longirostris

A variety of *Synodontis longirostris.*

A variety of *Synodontis longirostris.*

Synodontis acanthomias

Synodontis waterloti

A species similar to *Synodontis waterloti,*
but not as yet identified.

Synodontis schoutedeni

Synodontis schoutedeni

Synodontis alberti

Synodontis alberti

Synodontis greshoffi

Synodontis greshoffi

Possibly *Synodontis greshoffi*.

An unidentified *Synodontis*.

Synodontis robertsi

Synodontis leopardinus

Synodontis nigrita

Possibly *Synodontis nigrita*.

Synodontis ocellifer

Synodontis robbianus

A species similar to *Synodontis robbianus*.

12

An unidentified *Synodontis.*

An unidentified *Synodontis.*

An unidentified *Synodontis.*

Synodontis haugi

An unidentified
Synodontis.

An unidentified
Synodontis.

Synodontis multipunctatus

Synodontis multipunctatus

Synodontis eurystomas

Synodontis dhonti

Synodontis petricola

Synodontis granulosus

Synodontis njassae

Synodontis victoriae

Synodontis nigromaculatus

Synodontis afrofischeri

Chiloglanis deckenii

Euchilichthys guentheri?

Chiloglanis lukugae

Chiloglanis species

Chiloglanis species

16

Malapterurus
electricus

Malapterurus
electricus

Malapterurus
electricus?

Malapterurus
microstoma

Clarotes laticeps

Bagrus ubangensis

Lophiobagrus cyclurus

Chrysichthys ornatus

Chrysichthys longipinnis

Chrysichthys furcatus

Auchenoglanis occidentalis

18

Phyllonemus typus

Parauchenoglanis guttatus

Parauchenoglanis macrostoma

Schilbe mystus

Schilbe uranoscopus

Eutropiellus debauwi

Parailia longifilis

Heterobranchus longifilis

Clarias gariepinus

Clarias angolensis

Channallabes apus

Gymnallabes typus

***Amphilius* sp.**

Phractura intermedia

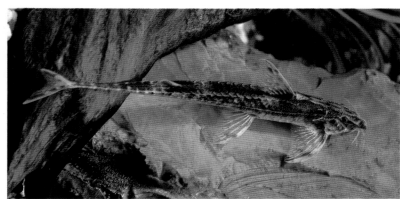

***Phractura* sp.**

Belonoglanis tenuis

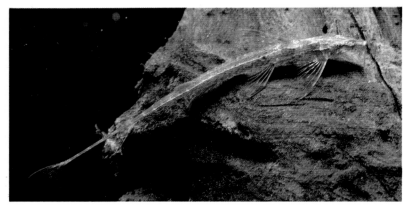

AUSTRALIA

Most of the few catfishes that live in the Australian continent, in contrast to those from other continents, have had their origins in the sea. The catfishes that live in the sea are the stinging catfishes (Plotosidae) and mouthbrooding catfishes (Ariidae). In Australia, the catfishes that belong to these families can be seen existing in either the sea or freshwater areas. There are also some species that originally developed in fresh waters and are restricted to them as well as others that come and go freely between the sea and freshwater areas.

Many of the catfishes that live in the sea are also distributed around the Asian continent and are therefore available to the local people in Japan. But some Australian freshwater catfishes are not imported into Japan. One of these is the famous "mouthbrooder" Australians call the big salmon or blue catfish (*Arius graeffei*). The fact that there are many eggs orally incubated by the male attracts the interest of people who study catfishes.

オーストラリア

Anodontoglanis dahli

22

Tandanus bostocki

Neosilurus glencoensis

Neosilurus sp.

Neosilurus sp.

Neosilurus sp.

Hexanematichthys leptaspis

Japan, China, and Europe (and also including a part of Africa).

One of the World's biggest catfishes, which is called the European wels *(Silurus glanis)*, belongs to the family Siluridae. Another giant catfish is the Amazon River's "paraiba." The length of the biggest catfishes so far recorded are about 5m long, and catfishes that are over 2m long exist in China. One of the largest catfishes is *Pangasianodon gigas*, which lives in the Mekong River and is over 3m in length, as well as having a weight of over 300 kg.

Japanese researchers are more interested in Japanese catfishes than Southeast Asian catfishes because they are geographically closer and therefore more easily

There are two main groups of catfishes in the Eurasian continent, the silurids (Siluridae) and the bagrids (Bagridae). These two families adapt very readily to changes in their environment. That is why they were capable of becoming widely distributed in tropical areas as well as in

obtainable and observable. The Southeast Asian studies are also covered with a mysterious veil and research on them doesn't progress as well as the studies on the Japanese catfishes because of the long political battles in the countries where they are found.

Silurus asotus

Silurus lithophilus

24

Silurus biwaensis

Silurus glanis

Silurodes eugeneiatus

Silurichthys hasselti

Ompok bimaculatus

Kryptopterus bicirrhis

Kryptopterus bicirrhis

Kryptopterus macrocephalus

Kryptopterus apogon

Wallago miostoma

Wallago leeri

Wallago attu

Belodontichtyhs dinema

26

Pelteobagrus nudiceps

Pelteobagrus ornatus

Coreobagrus ichikawai

Pseudobagrus fulvidraco

Heterobagrus bocourti

Pseudobagrus aurantiacus

Chandramara chandramara

Leiocassis siamensis

Leiocassis poecilopterus

Bagrichthys hyselopterus

Mystus micracanthus

Mystus vittatus

Mystus nemurus

Mystus wyckii

Bagrus sp.

Pangasius sutchi

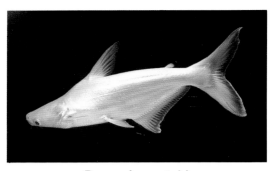

Pangasius sutchi

Paugasius sp.

Pangasius larnaudii

Pangasius sp.

Pangasius sanitwongsei

Bagarius bagarius

Bagarius sp.

Erethistes montana

Glyptothorax trilineatus

Glyptothorax major

Gagata schmidti

Gagata cenia

31

Chaca bankanensis

Heteropneustes fossilis

Clarias batrachus

Clarias batrachus

Clarias fuscus

Liobagrus reini

AMERICA

On the other hand, it is said that more than 1000 to 1500 different kinds of catfishes are in existence in the southern continent. It is often called the catfish Mecca. The most speciose families are the Pimelodidae, Loricariidae, Callichthyidae, and Doradidae. This is about half the amount of the total freshwater and marine catfishes known for the whole world. In these groups, some of them, such as the loricariids, are poorly

サウス アンド ノース アメリカ

According to the continental drift theory, it is said that both North and South America were separated 100 million years ago, although they are now joined together. Therefore, the same kind of catfishes can rarely be seen in both continents. Only a relatively few species of ictalurid (Ictaluridae) and ariid (Ariidae) catfishes are found in the northern continent.

classified, and there are other groups, such as the *Corydoras* catfishes of the family Callichthyidae, that are still being divided at present by (among others) investigations into their DNA.

The Amazon jungle, which has the greatest quantity of water and variety of habitats in the world, still has many undiscovered species of catfishes.

Pimelodus pictus

Pimelodus maculatus

Pimelodus maculatus

Pimelodus sp.

Pimelodus blochii

Pimelodus ornatus

Pimelodus albofasciatus

Pimelodus blochii

Pimelodella gracilis

Pimelodella linami

Pimelodella cristata

Pimelodella parnahybae

Rhamdia quelen

Rhamdia sp.

Imparfinis minutus

Rhamdella microcephala

Heptapterus sp.

Brachyrhamdia meesi

Brachyrhamdia sp.

Brachyrhamdia imitator

Brachyrhamdia rambarrani

Pseudopimelodus fowleri

Pseudopimelodus species

Pseudopimelodus raninus raninus

Pseudopimeldous raninus raninus

Pseudopimelodus

Pseudopimelodus raninus acanthochiroides

38

Pseudopimelodus zungaro

Pseudopimelodus zungaro

Pseudopimelodus zungaro

Pseudopimelodus albomarginatus

Microglanis iheringi

39

Microglanis

Paulicea lutkeni

Paulicea species

Paulicea lutkeni variety

Phractocephalus hemioliopterus

Perrunichthys
perruno

Leiarius pictus

Leiarius pictus

Platynematichthys notatus

Calophysus macropterus

Pinirampus
pirinampu

Brachyplatystoma
filamentosum
variety

Brachyplatystoma
filamentosum
variety

42

Brachyplatystoma filamentosum

Brachyplatystoma filamentosum

Brachyplatystoma filamentosum variety

Brachyplatystoma flavicans

43

***Brachyplatystoma
juruense***

Brachyplatystoma species

Brachyplatystoma vaillanti

Brachyplatystoma species

Duopalatinus species

Duopalatinus species

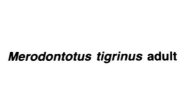

Merodontotus tigrinus juvenile

Merodontotus tigrinus adult

*Pseudoplatystoma
fasciatum*

*Pseudoplatystoma
tigrinum*

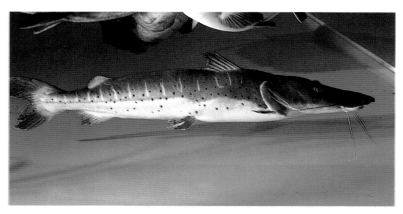

*Pseudoplatystoma
fasciatum* var.

*Pseudoplatystoma
coruscans*

Sorubim lima

Sorubim lima

Hemisorubim platyrhynchus

Hemisorubim platyrhynchus

Duopalatinus malarmo

Sorubimichthys
planiceps

Sorubimichthys planiceps

Goeldiella eques

Platystomatichthys sturio

Platystomatichthys sturio

Pimelodid species

Rineloricaria microlepidogaster

Rineloricaria microlepidogaster

Rineloricaria lanceolata

Rineloricaria fallax

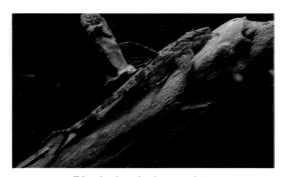

Rineloricaria lanceolata

Rineloricaria morrowi

Loricariichthys sp.

Loricariichthys sp. ?

Loricariichthys sp. ?

Ricola sp.

Pseudohemiodon sp.

Pseudohemiodon laticeps

50

Pseudoloricaria sp. ?

Spatuloricaria caquetae

Spatuloricaria caquetae

Pyxiloricaria sp.

Loricariichthys sp.

Hemiodontichthys acipenserinus

Loricariichthys sp.

Loricariichthys
sp.

Lamontichthys
sp.

Lamontichthys
filamentosus

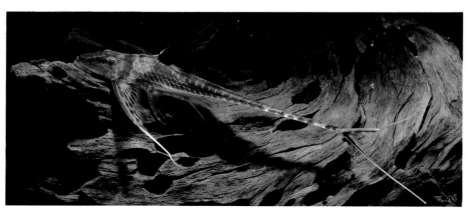

Lamontichthys
filamentosus

Sturisoma barbatum

Sturisoma aureum

Sturisoma aureum

Farlowella acus

Farlowella gracilis

Farlowella sp.

Hypostomus plecostomus

Hypostomus plecostomus

Hypostomus sp.

Hypostomus sp.

Hypostomus sp.

Hypostomus sp.

Hypostomus sp.

Hypostomus sp.

Hypostomus sp.

Hypostomus sp.

Hypostomus sp.

Hypostomus punctatus ?

Hypostomus sp.

Hypostomus sp.

Hypostomus sp.

Hypostomus sp.

Hypostomus

Hypostomus sp.

Hypostomus sp.

Hypostomus sp.

56

Hypostomus sp.

Hypostomus margaritifer

Hypostomus margaritifer var.

Hypostomus sp.

Hypostomus sp.

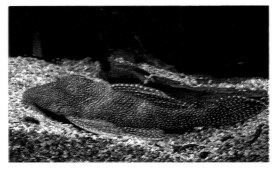

Hypostomus sp.

Pterygoplichthys gibbiceps

Pterygoplichthys gibbiceps var.

Pterygoplichthys gibbiceps var.

Pterygoplichthys sp.

Pterygoplichthys multiradiatus

Pterygoplichthys sp.

58

Pterygoplichthys sp.

Pterygoplichthys sp.

Pterygoplichthys anisitsi

Cochliodon cochliodon

Pogonopomoides parahybae

Pseudorinelepis sp.

Pseudorinelepis pellegrini

Ancistrus tamboensis

Ancistrus tamboensis

Ancistrus tamboensis

Ancistrus sp.

Ancistrus hoplogenys

Ancistrus sp.

Ancistrus sp.

Ancistrus **sp.**

Ancistrus **sp.**

Ancistrus **sp.**

Ancistrus temminckii

Ancistrus **sp.**

Lasiancistrus carnegei

Lasiancistrus carnegei **var.?**

61

Parancistrus aurantiacus

Parancistrus aurantiacus

Parancistrus aurantiacus var.

Parancistrus aurantiacus var.

Parancistrus sp.

Parancistrus aurantiacus

Parancistrus sp.

62

Parancistrus sp.

Parancistrus sp.

Parancistrus sp.

Chaetostoma wuchereri

Chaetostoma thomasi

Chaetostoma sp.

Lithoxus sp.

63

Peckoltia vittata

Peckoltia vittata var.

Peckoltia sp.

Peckoltia sp.

Peckoltia platyrhyncha

Peckoltia sp.

Peckoltia sp.

Peckoltia sp. cf. *brevis*

64

Peckoltia sp.

Peckoltia sp.

Peckoltia pulcher

Peckoltia sp.

Panaque nigrolineatus

Panaque nigrolineatus

Panaque nigrolineatus var.

Panaque sp.

Panaque albomaculatus

Panaque sp.

Panaque suttoni

Panaque suttoni var.

Panaque **sp.**

Acanthicus adonis

Acanthicus hystrix

Pseudacanthicus spinosus

Pseudacanthicus sp.

Pseudacanthicus sp.

Pseudacanthicus sp.

Pseudacanthicus sp.

Pseudacanthicus sp.

Pseudacanthicus sp.

Pseudacanthicus sp.

Pseudacanthicus sp.

Hypoptopoma thoracatum

Hypoptopoma guentheri

Hypoptopoma carinatum

Otocinclus arnoldi

Otocinclus affinis

Otocinclus nattereri

Otocinclus vittata

Otocinclus flexilis

70

Otocinclus paulinus

Parotocinclus maculicauda

Loricariidae sp.

Loricariidae sp.

Loricariidae sp.

Loricariidae sp.

Loricariidae sp.

Loricariidae sp.

Callichthys callichthys

Hoplosternum thoracatum

Hoplosternum thoracatum

Hoplosternum sp.

Hoplosternum pectorale

Hoplosternum pectorale

Dianema urostriatum

Dianema longibarbis

Hoplosternum littorale

Corydoras
punctatus
var.

C. Julii var.

C. Julii var.

C. trilineatus

C. trilineatus var.

74

Corydoras copei

C. leopardus

C. leopardus

C. agassizii var.

C. leopardus var.

C. agassizii

Corydaoras sp. cf. *agassizi*

C. ornatus

C. pulcher

C. ambiacus

Corydoras sp.

Corydoras sp.

C. orphnopterus

C. sychri

76

Corydoras atropersonatus

Corydoras sp.

Corydoras leucomelas

Corydoras sp. cf. *leucomelas*

C. melanistius

Corydoras sp. cf. *melanistius*

C. melanistius brevirostris

Corydoras sp. cf. *melanistius brevirostris*

Corydoras surinamensis ?

C. schwartzi

C. delphax

Corydoras sp.

Corydoras sp.

C. bicolor

Corydoras sp.

C. evelynae

Corydoras sp.

Corydoras sp.

C. loretoensis

C. xinguensis

79

Corydoras polystictus

C. polystictus

C. caudimaculatus

Corydoras sp.

C. reticulatus

C. reticulatus var.

C. sterbai

C. haraldschultzi

Corydoras **sp. cf.** *maculifer*

Corydoras **sp. cf.** *maculifer*

Corydoras **sp. cf.** *maculifer*

C. robineae

C. concolor

Corydoras aeneus

C. aeneus

C. aeneus

C. aeneus var. ?

C. melanotaenia

C. zygatus

C. rabauti

Corydoras potaroensis

C. panda

C. panda var.

C. melini

Corydoras melini var.

C. melini var.

C. metae

Corydoras arcuatus

C. arcuatus ?

Corydoras sp.

C. axelrodi

Corydoras sp. cf. *axelrodi*

C. habrosus

C. bondi bondi

C. bondi copenamensis

C. loxozonus

C. osteocarus

C. baderi

C. sanchesi

85

C. elegans

C. elegans var.

C. nanus

C. undulatus

86

Corydoras latus

C. latus

C. guapore

Corydoras sp.

C. hastatus

C. pygmaeus

Corydoras barbatus

C.   barbatus

C. ehrhardti

C. macropterus

C. macropterus

C. garbei

Corydoras sp.

88

Corydoras paleatus

C. paleatus

C. sp.

Corydoras sp.

C. nattereri

C. prionotus

Corydoras sp. cf. *prionotus*

Corydoras acutus

C. cervinus

C. pastazensis

C. semiaquilus

Corydoras ourastigma ?

Corydoras sp. cf. *blochi blochi*

C. blochi vittatus

C. blochi vittatus

C. fowleri

C. narcissus

C. simulatus

C. simulatus var.

Corydoras sp. cf. *simulatus*

Corydoras sp. cf. *simulatus*

C. amapaensis

C. amapaensis

C. ellisae

C. treitlii

C. stenocephalus

C. stenocephalus

Corydoras **sp.**

Corydoras **sp. cf.** *burgessi*

Corydoras **sp. cf.** *burgessi*

C. burgessi

C. adolfoi

C. imitator

Corydoras **sp.**

Corydoras **sp.**

Corydoras sp.

Corydoras sp.

Corydoras sp.

Corydoras sp.

Corydoras sp.

Corydoras sp.

Corydoras sp.

C. melanistius var. ?

94

Brochis multiradiatus

Brochis multiradiatus var.

Brochis britskii

Brochis splendens

Brochis splendens

Aspidoras   menezesi

Aspidoras pauciradiatus

Opsodoras sp.

Opsodoras ternetzi

Opsodoras sp.

Opsodoras stubeli

Opsodoras stubeli var ?

Platydoras costatus

Orinocodoras eigenmanni

Amblydoras hancocki

Amblydoras sp.

Acanthodoras spinosissimus

Acanthodoras spinosissimus

97

Agamyxis pectinifrons

Astrodoras asterifrons

Anadoras grypus

Anadoras regani

Liosomadoras oncinus

Liosomadoras   oncinus

Doradidae

Doradidae

98

Pterodoras granulosus

Pterodoras granulosus

Pterodoras granulosus

Megalodoras irwini

Megalodoras irwini

Lithodoras dorsalis

Lithodoras dorsalis

Pseudodoras niger

Rinodoras dorbignyi

Liosomadoras sp.

Trachydoras paraguayensis

Anduzedoras microstomas

100

Leptodoras linnelli

Opsodoras leporhinus

Hassar notospilus

Hassar sp.

Hasser iheringi

Auchenipterus thoracatus

Auchenipterus longimanus

Auchenipterus nuchalis

Parauchenipterus fisheri

Parauchenipterus fisheri

Parauchenipterus fisheri

Parauchenipterus galeatus

Parauchenipterus sp.

Parauchenipterus sp.

Parauchenipterus sp.

Parauchenipterus sp. ?

Tatia aulopygia

Tatia intermedia

Tatia neivai

Tatia reticulata

Tatia brunnea

Tatia sp.

Centromochlus heckeli

104

Pseudauchenipterus sp.

Trachelyopterichthys taeniatus

Entomocorus benjamini

Entomocorus sp. ?

Trachelyichthys exilis

Trachelyichthys exilis

Auchenipterus demeraral

Ageneiosus brevifilis

Ageneiosus sp.

Hypophthalmus sp.

Ageneiosus sp.

107

Platystacus cotylephorus

Platystacus cotylephorus

Aspredo aspredo

Bunocephalus coracoideus

Bunocephalus coracoideus

Bunocephalus kneri

Bunocephalus sp.

Agmus lyriformis

Agmus lyriformis

Bunocephalus sp.

Trichomycterus alternum

Trichomycterus sp.

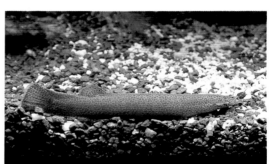

Eremophilus candidus

Eremophilus mutisii

Bullockia moldonadoi

Pseudosteogophilus nemurus

Plectrochilus erythrurus

Vandellia sp.

Pareiodon microps

Pareiodon sp.

Tridensimilis nemurus

Cetopsis sp.

Pylodictis olivaris

Ictalurus melas

Ictalurus punctatus

Ictalurus punctatus

Noturus flavus

Arius jordani

Arius seemanni

The catfishes contribute over 2,000 species to the 20,000 or so existing species of fishes in the world. We could therefore say that it is a big group in the entire fish "family." It is very difficult to grasp their situation, not only because of their numbers, but also because they are spread all over the world, especially in tropical areas.

There are many catfish lovers among biologists, because not only do they have so many attractive features but they also provide a wide range of information and are interesting subjects for study.

In this chapter we would like to review how wide the range is and how variable the catfishes are in morphology and ecology. There are no definite theories yet about relationships of the catfishes, but I would like to talk about the hypotheses that have already been established.

WHAT IS A CATFISH?

Generally speaking, most people think of catfishes as having a slimy body without any scales, as well as big heads and of course the famous whisker-like barbels, like those that are characteristic of typical Japanese catfishes. The people who know only the typically available Japanese catfishes would never dream that there is such a large variety of catfishes and that they could be distributed on all continents horizontally and vertically (i.e., from ground level to high mountains), except for the poles. For example, some of them are covered with armor-like plates, and some live in rapids using a sucker to maintain their position, although generally they live on the bottom in swamps. Some have bodies that are virtually transparent, some generate electricity, and some are parasitic upon others. It is still very enjoyable to watch them even though many are colorless.

The classification of catfishes is very difficult for the taxonomist. One of the reasons is that there are so many species and they have such a very wide distribution that it is not easy to grasp the whole picture. Moreover, the majority of catfishes are centered in tropical areas where people cannot get to them very easily. But some taxonomists have a lot of enthusiasm for studying catfishes and many biologists actually go to the Amazon and other remote places to search for them.

What is a catfish anyway? According to the taxonomists, catfishes have whisker-like barbels and are either naked (with no scales) or their bodies are covered with bony scutes. They may not have lower gill rakers. But there are always exceptions in this world, so we cannot easily provide a specific definition. There is only a rather vague, uncertain definition of catfishes at the present time.

Some earlier taxonomists have already tried to classify them. Berg, for example, divided them into 23 families; Chardon recognized 32 families, while some taxonomists (such as Greenwood, et al.) classify them into

Figure 1
LIST OF 31 CATFISH FAMILIES

Family Name	Range	Genera	Species
DIPLOMYSTIDAE	South America	1	2
ICTALURIDAE	North America	6	16
BAGRIDAE	Africa + Asia	27	205
CRANOGLANIDIDAE	Asia	1	3
SILURIDAE	Asia + Europe	15	70
SCHILBEIDAE	Africa + Asia	20	60
PANGASIIDAE	Asia	8	25
AMBLYCIPITIDAE	Asia	2	5
AMPHILIIDAE	Africa	7	47
AKYSIDAE	Asia	3	8
SISORIDAE	Asia	20	65
CLARIIDAE	Africa + Asia	13	100
HETEROPNEUSTIDAE	Asia	1	2
CHACIDAE	Asia	1	2
OLYRIDAE	Asia	1	4

114

Figure 1
LIST OF 31 CATFISH FAMILIES

Family Name	Range	Genera	Species
MALAPTERURIDAE	Africa	1	2
MOCHOKIDAE	Africa	10	150
ARIIDAE	N&S Amer + Asia + Australia	20	120
DORADIDAE	South America	37	80
AUCHENIPTERIDAE	Cen + S America	19	60
ASPREDINIDAE	South America	8	25
PLOTOSIDAE	Africa + Asia + Australia	8	30
PIMELODIDAE	Cen + S America	56	290
AGENEIOSIDAE	South America	2	25
HYPOPHTHALMIDAE	South America	1	1
HELOGENIDAE	South America	2	4
CETOPSIDAE	South America	4	12
TRICHOMYCTERIDAE	South America	27	175
CALLICHTHYIDAE	South America	8	110
LORICARIIDAE	South America	70	450
ASTROBLEPIDAE	South America	1	75

31 families. Currently, workers have been using Greenwood's taxonomic system for teleostean fishes, but as research progresses in the future, it could be changed again. (See *figure 1* for the 31 families.)

Most catfishes live in fresh water, except for some species of the families Plotosidae and Ariidae. But some members of these two families have returned to fresh water and live there as strictly freshwater fishes.

Catfishes are generally classified depending on whether there is an adipose fin or not, on the shapes of the pectoral and caudal fins, on the sharpness of the pectoral and dorsal fin spines, on the structure of the Weberian apparatus, on the shape and position of the swim bladder, on the shapes of muscles and bones, as well as on the number and position of each fin and on the relative proportions of each part of the body.

WHAT IS THE UPPER JAW MADE OF?

Let's start with the upper jaw, which is one of the important features. In the bony fishes the premaxillary bone bears the teeth as well as forms the edge of the upper jaw. In connection with this, the muscle that is attached to the main upper jaw bone makes that jaw move. In catfishes, that muscle has become modified in shape and makes the barbels move. There are also at the base of the barbels small bones that support the whiskers. What forms the catfish upper jaw is the premaxillary bone stretching along the entire mouth and bearing a large toothed surface. The premaxillary bone also forms the upper jaw in other fishes. But there is an exception. The catfishes of the family Diplomystidae, which live only in Chile and Argentina (South America), have teeth on the maxillary bone, which also operates as an upper jaw bone.

WHISKERS (BARBELS)

Catfish whiskers are famous and sometimes called the "catfish's moustache." Fully equipped catfishes have 8 barbels (four pairs), with 2 pairs on the upper jaw and 2 pairs on the lower jaw. But there are lots of different combinations regarding the number of whiskers. Some upper jaws have one pair of barbels while the lower has two pairs of barbels, or both upper and lower jaws have one pair each, while some catfishes have no barbels at all. Some Japanese catfishes have two pairs of barbels on both upper and lower jaws during their juvenile stages, but while they are still young they lose a pair of barbels. It is reported that the catfish barbel has numerous sensory pores that make it somewhat of a gustatory organ. It is a really useful sense for them to have. One might as well say that they have a "long tongue."

THE ADIPOSE FIN

Usually there are spines or rays that support the fin like the ribs of an umbrella. The adipose fin does not have the supporting spines or rays but is of the fleshy type and is placed behind the dorsal fin as if it were a second fin. We can also see the adipose fin in the salmons and trouts. There are many tetras that have an adipose fin, too. The adipose fin is a good character to use in classification. Twenty-two out of the 31 families that have been mentioned before have an adipose fin. Electric catfishes (Malapteruridae) do not have a dorsal fin but only an adipose fin. In some of the catfishes there is only a ridge that is barely discernible as an adipose fin, while in other catfishes the adipose fin is actually supported by fin rays. In *Corydoras* catfishes the adipose fin is preceded by a spine.

Most baby fishes that have just hatched have a continuous type of fin extending from behind the head to their vent around the caudal area (the finfold). As they grow, the dorsal, the caudal, and the anal fins are formed from this fin. The finfold selectively disappears, leaving the shape of each permanent fin. But the finfold in the adipose fin area remains and grows larger. Fishes with adipose fins are said to be, in general, primitive. This idea seems to have originated because the adipose fin is found in such relatively primitive groups as trout and salmon. It is not yet known at this point whether those catfishes that have an adipose fin are more primitive than the others or not.

THE DORSAL FIN

The shape of the dorsal fin varies from catfish to catfish. Some of them are normally shaped, with or without a spine, while the dorsal fins have completely disappeared in some groups, like the electric catfishes, family Malapteruridae. Normally, there are not many dorsal rays in most catfishes. Some dorsal fins, however, have a great number of fin rays. In the clariids, for example, the dorsal fin joins with the caudal fin and the number of fin rays may be close to a hundred. The plotosids have the anterior dorsal fin provided with a sharp spine. If a person gets stuck, it can be extremely painful. The posterior dorsal fin, with about 100 fin rays, follows behind and is completely joined to the caudal fin. On the other hand, some of the catfishes with a reduced or absent dorsal fin belong to the family Siluridae.

THE CAUDAL FIN
AND ITS VARIOUS SHAPES

The types of caudal fins of catfishes that are most commonly seen are rounded ones and those that are bifurcated. On the upper side of the bifurcated caudal fin of *Hypostomus* can be seen long filaments. Or, as in the case of the clariids and plotosids, the caudal fin and the anal fins are perfectly joined together.

It can be seen that there are fin rays radiating toward the outside in the caudal fin. At the base there is a triangular group of bones (the hypural plate) set up like a fan that supports these fin rays. These bones are said to be modified elements of spines of the vertebrae. The hypural plate

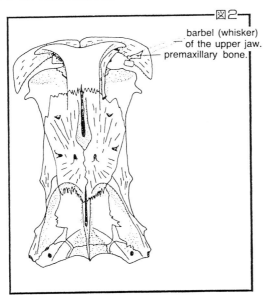

Figure 2. EUROPEAN CATFISH (Siluridae). A dorsal view of the cranium. In ordinary bony fishes, the premaxillary bone is the main bone of the upper jaw. In catfishes, it also supports the barbels (whiskers).

Figure 3. BAGRID CATFISH (CALLED GIGI BY JAPANESE). Illustration of the hypural plate. Catfishes have 6 basic tail bones in the hypural but 3-5 of the bagrid's hypural have begun to fuse.

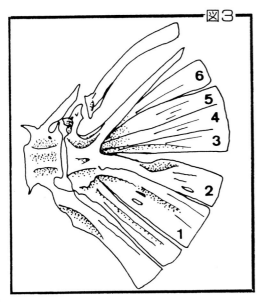

of catfishes was studied by Drs. Lundberg and Baskin. The basic structure (of the bony plate) is said to consist of 1-6 elements, which can be seen in the Bagridae (*figure 3*). But some of these elements, if not all of them, may be fused. There are a number of different types, but none of the hypurals are fused in the young.

The shape of the caudal fins of catfishes varies, e.g. rounded, bifurcated, etc. The hypurals of the lower hypural plate are also variously fused: nothing is fused; only the upper leaf is fused or only the lower leaf; or only parts of it are fused; etc.

The fishes with fused hypural plates are generally said to be good swimmers. But the fused hypural can be seen in *Chaca chaca* (family Chacidae) or the Plotosidae (see *figure 4*). It is not always appropriate to deduce the function directly from the existing form of a creature. We can't even imagine how useful the fused hypurals of *Chaca chaca* are since it is still a slow moving bottom fish. On the other hand, there is no completely fused hypural in the sea catfishes (family Ariidae), which are viewed as having good swimming ability.

SPINES OF THE DORSAL AND PECTORAL FINS

Some catfishes have strong bony spines derived from the first ray of the dorsal or pectoral fins. When they extend all their spines simultaneously, even small catfishes may become too big for carnivorous fishes to swallow them easily. On top of that, the tip of the spines are very sharp. This is one of the most useful defense systems for small fishes that are not very active and are prime targets for predation.

The catfishes have a locking system in their "shoulders" so that once the spines are erected they cannot be easily released unless it is done by the catfishes themselves.

Some catfishes can make sounds. Most of them make sounds by moving their pectoral fins. The young of the Mekong catfish (family Pangasiidae) that lives in the Mekong River is capable of making such a sound. Is the mature catfish with its three-meter-long body also capable of making sounds? If it does, it is hard to imagine how loud a sound they are capable of making with such a large body. The gigi (Pelteobagrus nudiceps) living in Japan makes a "Gi, Gi" warning sound when threatened by humans. But we do not know the function. I wonder if they use the sound in the water for communication between each other.

There are instances of catfishes having a saw-tooth edge or a projection on the front edge of the pectoral fin. In some cases, they have a smooth rear edge or a saw-tooth.

In Japan, the bagrids can be sexed by looking at this rear edge. This edge has well developed saw-teeth that become extremely big in the males but are slow to develop in the females.

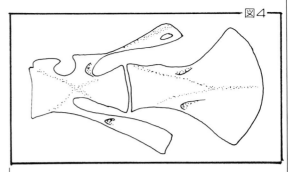

Figure 4. PLOTOSID CATFISH.
Illustration of the hypural plate. All the lower hypural bones have been fused.

Although there is a difference between males and females on this point, at the younger stages there is no difference. So it is thought this saw-tooth edge is useful for breeding activities. We don't know the function for sure. In the doradids and callichthyids, part of their spine is covered with small needle-like projections. In this case, it seems to be more effective for protecting themselves since additional spines make the predator lose some of its appetite.

Plotosids and amblycipitids have sharp dorsal and pectoral fin spines. It is very painful when we get stuck by them. There are poison glands below the fin that open to the surface. Because of the poison entering the wound caused by the sharp spines, a great deal of redness, swelling, and pain usually occur. Plotosids, especially, have a small hook-type spine on top of the dorsal fin spine. It is more painful to us when it (the hook) gets broken off in the wound. Both the poison and the spine are extremely effective for their protection.

Some species have the same type of spine and poison duct at the base of the pectoral fin. We feel considerable pain when we get stuck by it.

And there also are catfishes that have a spine in which the poison gland is centralized on top of its front edge and the poison is injected when it becomes stuck and broken off in the wound.

WEBERIAN APPARATUS

This organ was studied by Dr. Weber and consists of four small bones (tripus, intercalarium, claustrum, and scaphium) connected with the inner ear (see *figure 5*). It is said that the information coming through this organ does not include the direction of the information source because before it reaches the inner ear it goes through a common chamber where the right and left canals join together. Not only catfishes but also the other so-called Ostariophysi (characins, cyprinids, gymnotids) all have a Weberian apparatus.

It is said that the catfishes, compared with the other fishes, are more sensitive to sounds because of this organ. When the anterior swim bladder vibrates, these four small bones vibrate, causing the internal lymph sinus (sinus impar) to also vibrate and be able to detect the sound at that end. These strange but distinctly shaped bones look like small human ear bones. But

Figure 5. WEBERIAN APPARATUS. One of the species of Siluridae as seen from the rear. The figure to the right shows the relationship of the head bone, swim bladder and Weberian apparatus. The figure to the left shows the relationship between the 4 bones of the Weberian apparatus (tripus,intercalarium, scaphium and claustrum) and the maze of the inner ear.

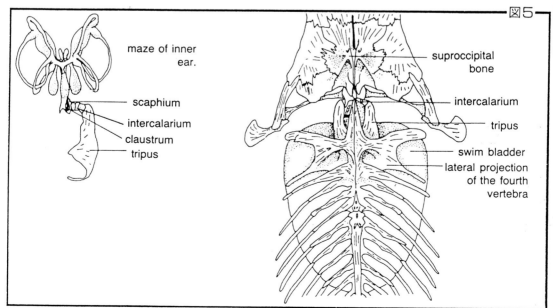

their origin is completely different. It is thought that the Weberian apparatus originated with the spinal column (vertebrae).

The Weberian apparatus of catfishes, compared with the other swimbladder group, is characterized by the tripus having extra parts at its posterior end (*figure 6*). However, the ones that have the simplest Weberian apparatus, for example callichthyids, have no extra parts.

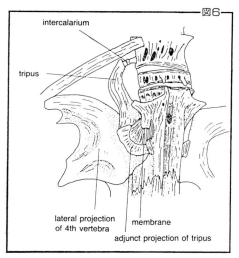

图6

intercalarium

tripus

lateral projection of 4th vertebra

membrane

adjunct projection of tripus

Figure 6: SILURID CATFISH VIEWED FROM THE VENTRAL SIDE. There is an adjunct projection behind the tripus. This point is firmly attached to the air bladder.

THE SWIM BLADDER IS NOT ONLY A FLOAT

The swim bladder is one of the most important organs of the catfishes. It is not only used for the adjustment of buoyancy but also as an accessory breathing organ, an amplification system for hearing (resonator), and also a sound producing system.

The shape of the catfish's swim bladder varies. It usually has one chamber but some of them, like the electric catfishes (family Malapteruridae) and *Pangasius* (family Pangasiidae), have two chambers. The external shape generally appears like a normal single-chambered swim bladder but internally it is divided into smaller compartments. Normally it is divided into anterior and posterior compartments by a thin membrane. But again it can sometimes be divided into left and right as well as rear compartments.

The big difference between the catfish swim bladder and that from any other fishes is that it is fixed firmly under the spinal column and encapsulated by a united structure involving flattened ribs dorsally. The 4th and 5th ribs expand like a butterfly's wings and surround the swim bladder. In extreme cases, for example *Callichthys* (family Callichthyidae), the swim bladder is so completely covered by ribs that it is very difficult to remove.

Though the shape of the swim bladder varies, e.g., oval, heart-shaped, and even some that are long and thin posteriorly, they are all positioned against the spinal column and above the stomach. Some of the silurid swim bladders extend as far as to the middle of the anal fin. Swim bladders of this kind, when the fish are still very young, start growing in an ordinary shape with a little bit of a sharp end to the oval. Some

Brochis britskii.

catfishes have an expanded swim bladder. In this case, there are many compartments and it is known that it works as an accessory organ for breathing. On the other hand, as with the case of the silurid catfishes, as the united structure is developed and becomes hard on the surface of the swim bladder, is it not likely working as an accessory organ for breathing? The silurid catfish that has this type of swim bladder has a big head and a thin body shape. From this point of view, we can imagine that the swim bladder may be working as a counterweight. If we could, we would ask the catfish.

As the swim bladder originally grows and expands as a part of the intestine, is it naturally connected with the intestinal tract by a thin duct? In some of the plotosids it has completely lost its flexibility after losing this duct and the swim bladder itself became more rigid. I wonder if there is a function that amplifies the sound with such a hardening of the swim bladder?

The origin of the lung of land vertebrates may have involved the swim bladder. Some of the present-day fishes are even now using it as an accessory organ for breathing. We can see this type for example in *Pangasius* (family Pangasiidae). Their swim bladders are flexible and are divided into small compartments with the walls of a foamy nature with many capillaries and other blood vessels surrounding it. But the swim bladder that is used as a lung is merely an accessory breathing organ; it is impossible for the fish to survive using the swim bladder alone.

The abdominal cavity is covered with muscles in ordinary fishes. But since the catfishes have no muscle surrounding the swim bladder it is actually closer to the information coming from the sound source. It is thought that the lateral muscles of the swim bladder have been lost to enable the catfishes to receive the sound waves more effectively. The swim bladder and Weberian apparatus work together continuously to amplify the sounds. The only effective external information sources for the nocturnal catfishes that live in muddy waters are sound and smell.

The *Callichthys* (family Callichthyidae) swim bladder is covered with a bony capsule. In general, the swim bladders are in the abdominal cavity which is located behind the head. This strange looking catfish that wears an external armor seems to have a capsule of bone in which there is the swim bladder. I wonder if the swim bladder even in this circumstance can possibly amplify the vibrations received and convey them to the Weberian apparatus.

THE MOST IMPORTANT FEATURES OF CLASSIFICATION: BONES AND MUSCLES

Although external features are important in order to classify catfishes, specially shaped head bones or muscles are equally as important or perhaps even more so. We have described here bones of the head and tail, as well as muscles that are found on the side of the head.

The skull in general consists of many bones. In some catfishes, the number of skull bones has decreased because of remarkable simplifications; in others their number has increased because the whole head appears as if it is covered with armor. One of the major common features is that there is neither the parietal nor the subopercular bones. We do not know for sure yet whether the former bone has been lost or simply united with another bone. When there is a missing bone, it is generally recognizable in those types of catfishes that are covered with armor. Various additional parts are needed because it is impossible to cover the whole head with a small number of bones. I wonder if the decrease of head bone elements in the catfishes has a connection with flat heads. On the other hand, the increase in elements seems to have a connection with the armor for the protection of the fish.

The skull protects the brain, which is the center of the nervous system of vertebrates. At the same time, it is a place for the attachment of the muscle that moves the jaws. The jaws provide the entrance for the energy to flow through in order to keep the animal working at its peak. That illustrates one of the most important features when we theorize on the evolution of the vertebrates. As with the catfishes, it sometimes happens that some of the externally similar appearing fishes have different arrangements and shapes of elements. On the contrary, some of the catfishes that look different externally sometimes have similar looking skulls. When this happens, the systematic taxonomist becomes totally delighted.

To compare one species of catfish with the other, we must find out which elements are homologous or have the same origin. But it is hard to compare catfishes to each other because the number of elements may have increased or decreased, and because we cannot see the difference from the shape and arrangement of the bony elements, especially in the cases where their elements have increased. We often cannot determine the origin of each and every bone.

One example of catfishes that have more elements composing the skull is *Clarias* (family Clariidae, *figure 7*). On the other hand, we can say that the catfish with fewer head bones originated in Japan and belongs to the family Siluridae. We can also say that the typical metamorphosis occurring due to

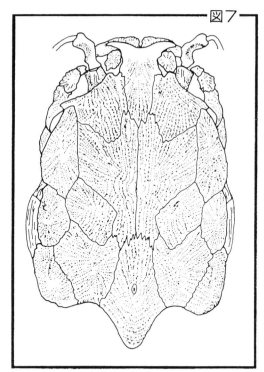

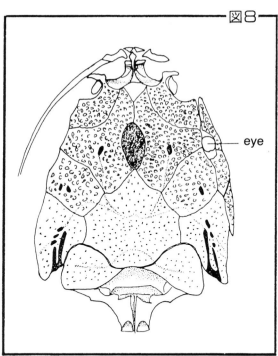

Figure 7. DORSAL VIEW OF SKULL OF CLARIID CATFISH. There are many lateral bones. (Gregory, 1954).

Figure 8. *CALLICHTHYS* sp. *(Family Callichthyidae).* Skull viewed from the dorsal side. Most of the head is covered with bone, except the eye.

Figure 9. PROJECTION OF OCCIPITAL BONE. One species of silurid with tent-like projection of the supraoccipital bone. Viewed from the side.

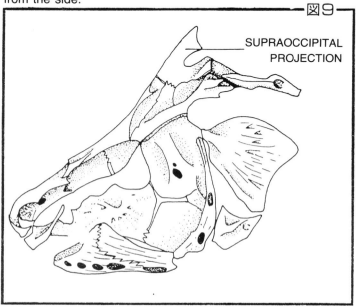

SUPRAOCCIPITAL PROJECTION

wearing the armor is seen in *Callichthys* (family Callichthyidae). In the case of *Callichthys*, the bones that cover the side of the head, the opercular bone, lachrymal bone, and preopercular bones, became expanded and the head is completely covered with bone (*figure 8*). The heads of catfishes are usually flat; when we see them from the back, sometimes they are completely flat. However, some projection develops from the front to the back in the middle of the skull (supraoccipital crest). To this is attached the lateral muscles that turn the body (*figure 9*). Now, about the muscle that attaches to the skull, on the lateral and ventral sides of the head there is the jaw muscle that mainly moves the lower jaw, and there is the body muscle on the posterior side of the skull that moves the body. I would like to talk about the muscle that moves the jaw here.

In the case of catfishes, the maxillary bone has become the base for the upper jaw barbels. The muscle that is attached to the bone that moves the jaw has lost its original function and has become the muscle that moves the barbels. This muscle is not always well developed despite the catfish having long and thick barbels; on the contrary, some catfishes have several thick muscles despite the weak-looking slender upper jaw barbels. In this case, it becomes possible to propose a good theory that they have become differentiated from ancestors that moved their barbels actively.

The jaw muscle that closes the lower jaw originates at the side of the skull and ends at the lower jaw. We can see various types of muscle layers. These are in turn divided into many layers, several layers becoming twisted, some quantities of muscle decreased, and a part of them becoming tendons.

OTHER FEATURES OF SHAPE

The relationships between the fin positions and the number of fin rays are good classificatory characteristics. These concern whether the pectoral fins reach to under the dorsal fin or not, whether the starting point of the anal fin reaches as far as the dorsal fin or not, etc., and are often used as guides to the classification of these fishes. But these concern whether the fin line evolved from more to less or the other way around and are not able to be characterized as a whole, because the direction of evolution is different in the different groups, although we can recognize a little tendency in the classified groups.

The proportion ratios of each part of the body are also used as guides to classification. By using these ratios, we can show the shape of the whole body in numbers, and make it easier to compare with others. For example, if we take the ratio of the length of the whole body to the length of the head, it shows that the head is bigger with a smaller ratio. But such ratios, just as the fin rays, seem to evolve in various directions in the classified groups, and it is hard to think about the unilateral direction of their evolution, such as from big to small or vice versa.

AIR BREATHING IN CATFISHES

I have already talked a little bit about the swim bladder. It can be seen that some catfishes can breathe air by using their swim bladder. For example, species of *Pangasius* (family Pangasiidae) that live in Asia do this. There are others that do not use their swim bladders to breathe air, but instead use a recently developed organ to breathe. They are the *Clarias* catfishes (family Clariidae), which includes the albino *Clarius* catfish, etc., that aquatic biologists are so familiar with. This type of catfish developed the accessory breathing organ that is called the upper gill organ or arborescent organ on the upper part of the gill. There is a cavity called the upper gill chamber between the second and third gill arches that is filled with these special structures. The catfishes suck the air in through the mouth when they come up to the water surface and dive again after they have filled the upper gill chamber with fresh air. Therefore *Clarias* can live in water that contains little oxygen, and can walk with twisting body motions a hundred meters over the ground by using their pectoral fin spines. Although the gouramis are not catfishes, 60%

of their breathing depends on the upper gill organ. So it is unusual when the water is made unbreathable for the fish to die from lack of air. We don't know what percentage of their arborescent organs the *Clarias* catfish rely on for their breathing, but if it is a high percentage, like that of the gouramis, they will probably also be able to utilize enough atmospheric air to survive.

With others, the digestive tract also acts as an accessory breathing organ. The *Callichthys* catfishes (family Callichthyidae) mostly have thin, highly vascularized intestines enabling them to take up oxygen freely. Such a fish can survive with little oxygen but they die if their breathing organs get shut down as with the gouramis. They rely on air breathing that much.

These air-breathing catfishes get the oxygen from the air even if there is an ample supply of oxygen in the water. But in any air-breathing fish, the carbon dioxide is exhaled into the water. Because the absorption coefficient of carbon dioxide in the water is very high, they use less energy exhaling it into the water than into the air.

ELECTRIC RECEIVER AND GENERATOR

The organ that receives the electrical signal from the outer world is present in all kinds of catfishes, although there is a difference in its development rate. With this organ, they can find their position in the muddy water and also locate food and prey. In addition, they can generate the electricity to electrify the area and find out the exact position of their prey when close by. It is very advantageous when protecting themselves from the enemy or for catching prey to also give them a shock. But there is a limited number of fishes that can do such things—only seven families in all fishes. These include the gymnotoids, the electric rays, the electric catfishes, the elephantnoses, etc. I will explain a little more about those fishes such as the electric catfishes.

Generally, it is said that the electric generating organ of these fishes originates in the muscle from both the embryological or from the anatomical point of view. The flat plate of various nucleus cells, so-called electric plates, originated in the muscle cells, piling up neatly and creating a battery in the body. Electric rays have a surprisingly large number of over 200,000 electric plates piled up. An ordinary muscle cell contracts by receiving an impulse, but such an electric plate generates electricity when it receives an impulse. Electric rays can generate over 200 volts and 2,000 watts, while electric catfishes can generate over 600 volts. This kind of large capacity electrical voltage is used to catch prey, but weak electrical discharges operate as a radar receiver that the lateral line organ transforms into necessary information about the predator or prey.

It is an ordinary generating system, with little difference from the electric ray. The electric catfish has a thin generating system right under the skin that surrounds the whole body and contains many electrical plates but it does not pile up. Also as those are too close to the skin it is doubtful whether or not the system originated in the muscle. It is thought that it might be a transformed gland system.

PROPAGATION ACTIVITY

Recently, various animal breeding activities have been observed and reported by ethological studies. Interesting reports have been done on catfishes. One of the interesting examples is that of *Synodontis* species (family Mochokidae). They lay their eggs in the mouths of cichlids that are known for their mouthbrooding. One catfish living in Tanganyika sprays its eggs into the mouth of the *Ophthalmotilapia* cichlids when the *Ophthalmotilapia* lays her eggs and incubates them in her mouth. On top of that, when both species' eggs have hatched in the mouth, the catfish fry also eat the *Ophthalmotilapia* cichlid's fry after they have used up their own yolk and grown large enough. This seems to be a ridiculous waste of time and much trouble for the *Ophthalmotilapia* cichlid which is left with the synodontid eggs and fry to brood. But I wonder if it is really trouble for the *Ophthalmotilapia* or not? I wonder even if the

Ophthalmotilapia notices the events happening in her mouth? What is she going to do when she realizes this problem? These are some of the questions that need to be solved in studies to be done in the future.

Some catfishes take care of their fry faithfully. The plotosid catfishes (family Plotosidae) are known for the males protecting their eggs. The plotosids can often be observed protecting their eggs in the field and it is actually the male plotosid catfish that is doing this. He excavates the sandy ground under the rocks to make a place for spawning. In an experiment conducted in an aquarium, it was found that both the male and female can build a nest. However, it is thought that mainly the male constructs the spot in the natural habitat because he can do it more skillfully and more efficiently than the female. The spawned eggs are generally heatedly protected by the male. The male plotosid diligently propels fresh water over the eggs with his pectoral fins, trying to keep them and the nest clean. They take care of their babies continuously until they leave the nest after they use up their yolk.

It is said that the males of *Amblyceps* species (family Amblycipitidae) and bagrid catfishes (family Bagridae) also protect their eggs, but detailed observations have not yet been made.

One particular member of the bagrid family lives in Lake Malawi in Africa and it is known that both parents cooperate in the care of the baby fish. The male catfish brings the food and ejects it out of his gills to feed the young. The female, on the other hand, spawns the eggs and also participates in the feeding of the young. It is very rare for a fish to act like this. This catfish is also interesting as the parents cooperate in the protection of their babies with a cichlid. Doing so, the catfish babies have a lower mortality rate with regard to predators. At the same time the cichlid also develops security. This brings good results for the both of them.

It is known that the sea-born ariid catfishes (family Ariidae) incubate their eggs in their mouth. However, this may not be completely accurate information because this hypothesis was formed after fry (newly hatched) and eggs were found in the mouth of the adult catfish. But it is hardly enough information on which to base a full hypothesis and know the exact ways in which the catfish incubate their eggs and hatch them.

However, propagation is easily observed in the *Corydoras* catfish (family Callichthyidae). Their spawning habits are usually known from fishes that are kept in aquaria. These charming armored catfishes do not look after their young. Females carry the fertilized eggs by holding them with their pelvic fins and placing them on some substrate such as plants. There is a theory that the female collects the sperm with her mouth from the male because the female places her mouth in the vicinity of the male's genital opening during the spawning act. The female then blows the sperm over the eggs by herself; but it is not proven and it is not sure when the eggs are actually fertilized.

Once in a while we can observe Japanese catfishes of the family Siluridae in the field after a heavy rain in the rainy season. Their spawning movements are interesting. The male coils himself around the female like a tire and lets the female spawn. The Japanese catfishes *Silurus asotus, S. lithophilus,* and *S. biwaensis* all go through this type of spawning act. Others, like the *Clarius* catfishes (family Clariidae), are observed going through the same type of spawning act in an aquarium.

The spawning activities of the catfishes are very interesting because, as with the different types of catfishes, there are many different spawning types within this group. This is the area where the most information and observational data will be recorded from now on.

DISTRIBUTION AND RELATIONSHIPS OF THE CATFISHES

Although the catfishes encompass 31 families and there is an uncertain relationship among them, their vast distribution makes us very curious when we think about their relationship with the ostariophysans. Let me talk about the classification of the Ostariophysi here.

The Ostariophysi is characterized by having a Weberian apparatus. According to Fink & Fink's 1981 classification (as well as some others) they are divided into the gonorynchiforms, cypriniforms, characiforms, and siluriforms. Those that concern us most here are the siluriforms and the gymnotiforms. The distribution of these groups currently is known.

The characiforms are distributed in South America and Africa, the cypriniforms are in Eurasia and North American, the siluroids are found in all four continents, and the gymnotoids are found in both Central and South America. Their relationships are indicated in *figure 10* according to Fink & Fink's (and others) theories. They indicate that the age of the catfishes's origin is not as old as that of the characiforms or the cypriniforms, having referred to the appearance of fossil otoliths of the family Ariidae in the beginning of the Cretaceous period, millions of years ago.

It is said in passing generally that characiforms have made their appearance before the Gondwana supercontinent separated from the South American continent, that is the Jurassic.

On the other hand, Fink & Fink do not agree with their own theory by reason of classificatory system differential at all.

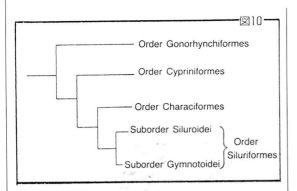

図10

- Order Gonorhynchiformes
- Order Cypriniformes
- Order Characiformes
- Suborder Siluroidei
- Suborder Gymnotoidei
} Order Siluriformes

Figure 10.CLASSIFICATION AND RE-LATIONSHIPS OF THE OSTARIO-PHYSI. (Fink & Fink, 1981).

Novacek & Marshall's theories, however, are very attractive. According to their 1976 classification, the Ostariophysi are divided into three major groups, the gonorynchiforms, the cypriniforms, and the siluriforms.

The order Cypriniformes includes the Characoidei and the Cyprinoidei; the Characoidei includes the Characoidea and the Gymnotoidea. They speculate that the relationships are as shown in *figure 11*. They explain that these differences in age are connected with the continental movements (*figure 12*).

In other words, before the Gondwana supercontinent became divided the ancestral ostariophysans evolved in both the South American and the African continents. Then the Ostariophysi differentiated in South America toward the

beginning of the Cretaceous period which started with the beginnings of the South Atlantic Ocean. The Cypriniformes and the Siluriformes were separated in the middle of the Cretaceous; they developed apart in South America and western Africa. During the time when the Atlantic Ocean was just about to form, these two continents had a common fauna regarding the catfishes and the cypriniforms. The Gymnotoidea became differentiated from the ancestors of the South American Characiformes.

Furthermore, the ancestor of the suborder Characoidei started spreading out. Toward the end of the Cretaceous and in the beginning of the Paleocene the once unified South American and African continents became separated. The Siluriformes and the Characoidea spread throughout the entire African continent.

Then the suborder Cyprinoidei originated from the fish that were analogized with the Characoidea. In the age of the Paleocene, at the same time of the closing of the Tethys Sea, the suborder Cyprinoidei and the order Siluriformes came into Europe.

From the last part of the Paleocene to the Miocene, the Tethys Sea opened up again and separated the African continent from the Eurasian continent. The suborder Cyprinoidei has evolved on its own in Europe. Thus the Siluriformes and the Cypriniformes have evolved from

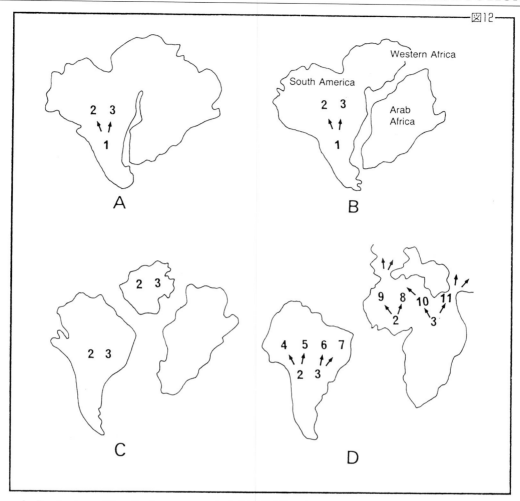

A: Beginning of the Cretaceous period. B: Middle of the Cretaceous period. C: Middle and late Cretaceous. D: Late Cretaceous - Dawn of the New World. 1: Ancestry type Ostariophysans. 2: Primitive Characiformes. 3: Primitive Siluriformes. 4: Electric eel, suborder Gymnotoidei. 5: South American Characoids. 6-7: South American Siluroids. 8: African Characoids. 9: Order Cypriniformes. 10-11: The Old World Catfishes.

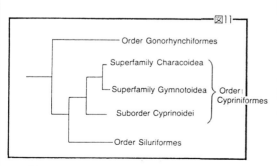

Figure 11.CLASSIFICATION AND RELATIONSHIPS OF THE OSTARIOPHYSI. (Novacek & Marshall, 1976)

their own fauna in the African and the Eurasian continents.

This hypothesis, which depends on the continental drift theory, has become a strong persuasive force by adding chronological information.

But compared with Fink & Fink's theory which was described before, we realize that the classificatory system itself is very different. Novacek &

Marshall, for example, divided the Cypriniformes into the suborder Characoidei and the suborder Cyprinoidei and put the Characoidea and the Gymnotoidea into the suborder Characoidei.

But Fink & Fink make the Cypriniformes and the Characiformes more independent, and also divide the Siluriformes into the suborder Gymnotoidei and the suborder Siluroidei. The biggest difference between them is the way the gymnotid group is dealt with. On top of that, there are even differences in which the second one thinks the origin of the catfish group is not as old as the Cypriniformes and the Characiformes.

In addition to this there is Dr. Darlington's hypothesis that the Characiformes originated in tropical Asia, and their dispersion has proceeded through the Bering land bridge, furthermore spreading into South America and completing their movement in the North American continent.

It is very interesting that the spreading of the ostariophysan group including the Siluriformes seems to have a deep relationship with the historical continental movement as each continent has its own features.

Lets concentrate on the suborder Siluroidei. Dr. Roberts's conjecture is as follows:

Suborder Siluroidei is distributed over all the continents of the earth with the equator at its center. In these areas, the South American continent produced the most families (13) and has an especially large number of species compared with the 9 families in the Eurasian continent and 8 families in the African continent. This abundance in South America probably occurred after the Andes Mountains were formed.

Up to now we have been talking about the remarkable shapes and habits of the catfishes, but they have a tremendous variety. Catfishes also have a remarkably large distribution. As we have said before, there are few studies that cover the entire catfishes, for example Chardon's swim-bladder research (1968) and Weber's comparative anatomy. Would it be too difficult for one researcher to cover the entire group of catfishes because of its huge extent?

Now let's refer to Dr. Chardon's conclusions based on his studies. Chardon put Fink & Fink's Siluroidei into the Siluriformes and divided it into three groups. These groups are based on the united condition of the vertebrae, and whether the shoulder zone is movable against the cranium or not. On top of that, these groups are further divided with three more groups: whether the swim bladder is free, degenerative but free, or if it is enclosed in a bony capsule. Within these nine divisions he divided the four main subgroups into 32 families (Chardon classified the Siluriformes into 32 families because he considered the Astroblepinae, which is a subfamily of the Loricariidae, as a full family). Some of them, of course, are intermediate or transitional stages. According to this conclusion, the seven subgroups that Chardon recognized as the *Diplomystes* subgroup (1 family), the silurid subgroup (3 families), the electric catfish (1 family), the bagrid subgroup (19 families), the cetopsid subgroup (1 family), the hypophthalmid subgroup (1 family), and the loricariid subgroup (6 families), are thought to have evolved, based on the diplomystid subgroup, to the third stage or the loricariid subgroup and the bagrid subgroup through the middle stage of the electric catfish and the cetopsid subgroup (*figure 13*). But there is a question whether these seven subgroups are monophyletic or not, especially the bagrid subgroup which has many families and a large distribution. Therefore, Dr. Chardon's phylogenetic presumptions are shaky on that basis. However, when we take an overall view of the whole suborder Siluroidei, there are only a few complete studies on the systematic relationships. This is why we have no other way except to use Dr. Chardon's systematic theory.

Although the paper is somewhat old now, Regan described the systematic relationships of the suborder Siluroidei based on comparative anatomy. According to this study, the Diplomystidae has retained the most general shape in the catfish group and is the most primitive. The same opinion is held by other researchers because the Diplomystidae has a simple structure of the Weberian apparatus and retains the characteristic of the catfish ancestor which has teeth on its maxillary bone. Regan placed the family Ariidae and the family Doradidae close to the Diplomystidae. The family Ariidae are the sea catfishes and are widely distributed in the tropical and subtropical seashore areas around the equator. We can think of the family Siluridae and the family Plotosidae as the next most primitive. These two families can be considered as being primitive because they have many ventral fin rays. Despite that feature, these two seem to have an advanced specialization because they have an extremely long caudal fin. As a more advanced group in the classification, the family Bagridae comes next. Then the North American Ictaluridae and many of the families of the Old World follow. The Callichthyidae and Loricariidae are considered specialized types.

In some of these famies, the relationships are checked closely and compared anatomically. For example, there are a number of theories that the Plotosidae and the Siluridae have a close relationship anatomically or that

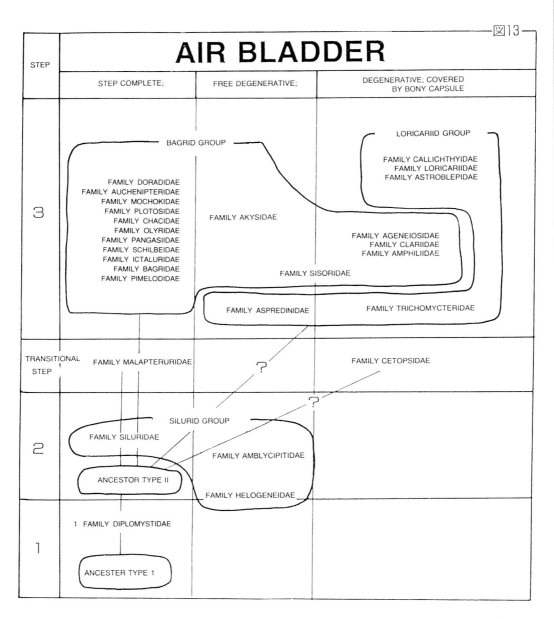

Figure 13. THE RELATIONSHIP OF SILURIFORMES ACCORDING TO CHARDON (1968). STEP I: The shoulder (humeral) zone is movable against the skull; the fifth vertebra is joned to the sixth vertebra. STEP II: Basically, the same as Step I, but the fifth vertebra is united with the fourth vertebra inside. STEP III: The shoulder (humeral) zone is firmly attached to the skull and the skull is united with the fifth vertebra.

the family Siluridae and the family Malapteruridae may have a close relationship because of the structure of the abdominal muscles.

Although catfishes make taxonomists cry because of this, you can say it is an attractive group because there are so many new doors to be opened and so many researchable subjects.

HOW TO RAISE CATFISHES

The catfishes we will discuss in this chapter are distributed in the world's fresh waters (although some may be able to travel from the rivers to the sea). Therefore, the same method cannot be used to raise all of them. The method of keeping and raising a catfish varies with its size, its shape, and of course the species involved. I am more comfortable in talking about the method of raising catfishes than the anatomy or systematics.

HOW TO RAISE THE BIG CATFISHES WITH THE PURPOSE OF KEEPING THEM FOR A LONG TIME

Big catfishes are tough fishes that everybody can raise if enough space and food are provided. However, many people still forego raising the big catfishes. "It grew too big to handle," and "They are too rough to put with other fishes in the same aquarium," are only two of the many reasons commonly given for avoiding them. Although they may look cute as young fish, the larger catfishes will grow big some day, a situation that must sooner or later be faced and handled by the aquarist.

The big catfish's real attraction to some aquarists is because it does grow big, and it is also attractive because of its rough nature. Like many big fishes, some people start raising them because they appear so cute at first glance when they are very young. But, fortunately, it is not necessary to prepare a large aquarium from the beginning. Starting with a small aquarium for the baby fish and enjoying their growing process by changing their aquarium to a larger size is one way of raising them.

But foresight and planning are necessary in order to prepare sufficient facilities for future use as these fishes are raised. You must not raise them by halves. You must start raising them with plans for keeping them for a long time.

An Aquarium Bigger than 120 cm is Needed in the End

It is generally better to prepare a tank bigger than 120 cm for the big catfishes. Some of them may even need a 180 cm aquarium. The aquarium has to have enough depth and height along with its width. As some of the big catfishes do not have much body flexibility, sufficient space must be provided so that they can turn freely in the tank.

Sometimes they get injured as they bash themselves into the glass sides of the aquarium; there are even cases when they have broken the glass. It is better, therefore, if the tanks are made of a thick acrylic material. Besides this, a thick, weighted lid is necessary to prevent them from jumping out of the tank.

A Top Filter is Necessary When One Takes into Consideration the Fish's Activity

Most catfishes are nocturnal. There is no exception with the big catfishes. Moving actively at night, they dig the bottom sand up and move it around. This kind of behavior and character

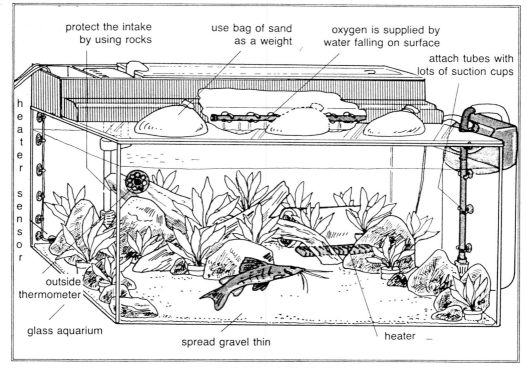

protect the intake by using rocks

use bag of sand as a weight

oxygen is supplied by water falling on surface

attach tubes with lots of suction cups

heater sensor

outside thermometer

glass aquarium

spread gravel thin

heater

CATFISH AQUARIUM

can affect the facility of raising the big catfishes if they continue to dirty the clean water.

The bottom filter has difficulty in working properly because of the sand being moved all around the tank. That is why we use the top filter or an outside power filter for the filtration. On top of this, it will be necessary to use two pumps together or to combine the different filters in order to increase filtration power. If one decides to use a top filter or canister filter, the sand at the bottom is not necessary at all.

Many of the big catfishes eat a lot and produce a great deal of excrement. Many of the leftover foods quickly rot. When these get mixed up into the sand, it makes the water quality worsen rapidly. Besides, it is easier to clean the tank up without sand when changing the water.

Protect the Equipment so It Will Not Be Broken

Sometimes the various pieces of equipment set up in the aquarium are broken by the activities of the catfishes. For example, the bi-metal system thermostat or the heater may happen to be bitten and the filter intake strainer may be knocked off when the catfishes turn and hit it with a part of their body. That is why the equipment must be protected to prevent accidents by proper design of the layout.

The strainer on the intake of the power filter should be protected by placing it between the rocks so that the catfish's body does not hit it. It should also be fixed firmly. The thermometer as well should be fixed securely, not only on the upper part of the glass but also on the lower part. Or use a liquid crystal thermometer which can be attached to the outside of the glass surface.

The thermostat should be an electronic one instead of the bimetal system one, and the sensor should be mounted securely and be hidden in the rocks. The heater should be fixed in the rocks and attached with a heater cover (available commercially).

Plan Your Layout so as Not to Harm the Catfishes

Most big catfishes rest during the day. It is better, therefore, to provide a quiet and peaceful resting environment. It is necessary that the design include sufficient hiding places and territory markers because many species have a strong consciousness about their own territory. Make some secretive places that they can use through driftwood and rock arrangements. During this operation, however, be sure to use rounded rocks and driftwood with rounded corners so

Protection is gained by planting heavily along the sides of the aquarium.

that the fishes are not harmed during their nightly activities.

From the esthetic point of view, decorate your aquarium with aquarium plants. Unfortunately, in most cases they are uprooted by the catfishes. They will be safe when the catfishes are still young, but quite often those plants are ruined, even if they are in a pot, when the catfishes mature. It will be necessary for them to be well protected with rocks, etc. It will be all right to use floating plants for the surface of the water.

Keep the Water Clean and the Temperature Low

The big catfishes, except for a few special types, can be raised in slightly acid or neutral water. It is better if the sand used in the filtration compartment is comparatively fine sand. In addition to this, put wool-type material into the aquarium filter for physical filtration and it is better to put the charcoal into the filter at the beginning. The special types are those catfishes that live in coastal areas. The water for them should be made weakly alkaline (pH 7.5-7.8) by using coral sand or silica sand.

As many of the catfishes live on the bottom, the proper water temperature for them is a little lower than for the catfishes that live in the upper areas near the surface. Generally speaking, the water temperature should be 22-23°C. But when new catfishes are added, raise the temperature to about 25°C, and as the fishes settle down gradually lower the temperature. Usually 25°C will be all right to raise them, but there will be trouble if a deadly disease begins to spread. Basically, it is better to raise catfishes at the lower temperatures.

Beware of Parasites and Scratches

The large species of catfishes commonly have scratches caused during transportation. It is better to give them a medicated bath when they are brought from the shop as there are many "invisible" scratches that could easily become infected.

Some individuals right after importation also have parasites. Precaution is required when feeding as well for some parasites may be introduced with raw food. The catfish with a parasite on its gill or body exhibits restless swimming, sudden violent movements, irregular and severe gill movements, staying on one spot where there is a current. As many of the parasites are invisible when these behaviors occur, implying a need for preventative measures, put in a 1/3 to 1/4 quantity of regular parasite extermination medicine (commercially available in pet shops) and wait and observe closely. Add 1/3 more if the same behavior continues one day after. Caution: many chemicals that are harmless to scaled fishes can be deadly to naked catfishes. Check with your dealer before using any chemicals in the catfish aquarium.

The catfishes appear to like old water, but as a matter of fact the opposite is true. It is easy for them to damage their skin as the water quality goes down, and sometimes they get sick from that. Their eyes turning white,

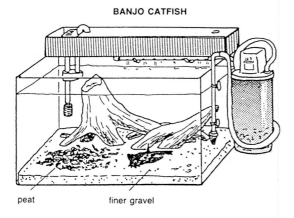

BANJO CATFISH

peat   finer gravel

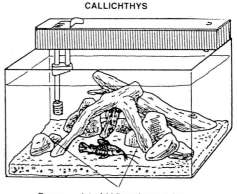

CALLICHTHYS

Prepare a lot of hiding places using driftwood and rocks.

the mucous membranes swelling, the mouth exhibiting festering red sores, the tips of the barbels disintegrating, are some of the symptoms commonly shown. Keep changing 1/3 of the water every 2 to 3 days and see what happens.

Catfishes are sensitive to medicines for fish diseases because usually they have a naked skin. We therefore cannot give them a large amount of medicine as it could become a deadly poison once they get sick and weak. It has to be done separately with less quantity than the prescription. With higher water temperatures it is also necessary to have strong aeration. It will be risky to raise the water temperature higher than 26°C. Some catfishes can even die due to the high water temperatures because many of them are just not able to adapt.

Do Not Let
Leftover Food Deteriorate
the Water Quality

Live foods, such as killifishes and minnows, goldfish, shrimp, etc., are better for the catfishes. The dynamic scene of the chase and the catching of the living food is one of the attractions of raising large catfishes. Microworms or glassworms are given when they are still small (just hatched). The person who cannot feed them live foods for reasons of sensitivity may substitute thawed frozen pond smelt, fish flesh, sausage, koi pellets, etc. Let them gradually get used to the fish flesh or sausage by feeding it when they

are hungry. But some of them, unless they are omnivorous, do not eat pellets designed for feeding carp.

When feeding in the evening the aquarium should be cleaned the next morning so that the water quality does not deteriorate. Take precaution with the quantity of food. Sometimes the catfish regurgitates the food if it overeats, polluting the water. During the raising process it is important to get the proper quantity and quality of food to the catfish.

Try Not to Mix
Nocturnal and Diurnal Fishes

Although many people keep the big catfishes with the arowana or big cichlids, etc., they should take some initial precautions because of the problems that may occur due to their opposite hours of activity. The catfishes start their activity at night and often crash into or bite the diurnal fishes. In such a case the diurnal fishes becomes stressed even though they are not bitten or chewed up.

Make good observations as to whether or not there are traces where the fishes were picked on, especially around the fins or on the skin. If there is such evidence, it is necessary to move either one or the other into another aquarium.

Some types of catfishes do not have much trouble with swimming with others except the sailfin catfish, the yellow sailfin catfish, and the catfishes that like swimming a lot (the glass catfish, the spotted catfish,

GLASS CATFISH

outlet for
undergravel
filter

Keep several
to form a
small school.

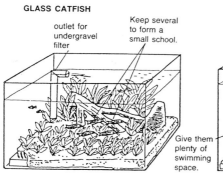

Give them
plenty of
swimming
space.

SCHILBEID CATFISH

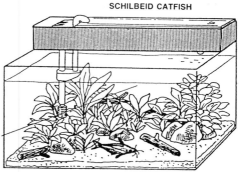

Pinirampus catfish, etc.). But if different types of catfishes, as the pimelodus catfishes or the redtail catfish, often pick on the others, precautions are necessary. On the other hand, the quiet catfishes (the spindle catfish, the sturgeon catfish, etc.) often become the target of the pickers.

How to Raise Very Active Types of Catfishes

Many of the big catfishes suddenly dash into the glass surfaces of the aquarium when frightened by something. Many of those that have a long or flat snout and an aerodynamic body are dashers. The piraiba catfish, the dourada catfish, and the tiger shovelnose catfish are typical ones. This kind of catfish sometimes not only can hurt their mouth by dashing about and bumping into things but they may even also break through the glass.

It is better to raise this type of catfish in a round aquarium to prevent the harmful dashing about but these cost a lot of money. So we have to rely on the design of the layout. First use an acrylic aquarium as it is less fragile. Although we make shel-

ters by using driftwood and rock settings, also make as large a space as possible for them to swim around in, and plant bushy plants along both sides and the back of the tank. The plants work like shock absorbers when the catfish crashes into them.

As typical plants, use the Amazon sword or giant vallisneria which are tall and tough. Support them by putting rocks firmly around the roots in the instances where there is a sandy bottom. If there is no sand at the bottom, place a vinyl sheet down even if it does not look good.

Also pay proper attention to the place where the aquarium sits. Try to put it in a quiet place where fewer humans are coming and going.

HOW TO RAISE THE MIDDLE AND SMALL SIZED CATFISHES

Many of the catfishes around the world belong to this middle or small size group, but in this chapter I would like to talk about those that haven't yet already been discussed. For example, the chaca catfishes, the callichthyids (except for

Corydoras species), the wood-cats, the pimelodids, all from South America, the glass cat-fishes, the bagrids of Southeast Asia, and the schilbeids of Africa.

The Family Chacidae— Gentle and Easy to Raise

Catfishes of the family Chacidae (located in Southeast Asia) have a body that looks like a rock or fallen leaf. They usually stay still at the bottom of the tank during the day but when the night comes they start to move about in the water looking for food. They like soft acid water but they are very adaptable. They can even tolerate a temperature range of 22-28°C. They like to eat everything, especially tubificid worms.

It is said that they lay their eggs on flat rocks and they sit down on top of the eggs to protect them until they hatch. They have a gentle nature, so it is possible for them to live together with other fishes smaller than the size of their mouth. They

Callichthyid catfishes making a foam nest prior to spawning.

bury themselves under the sand most of the time so coarse sand is not suitable for them. Also, it is a good idea to put a larger amount of peat into the aquarium.

The Callichthyid Catfishes that Make a Foam Nest

Their body is covered with hard plates. Species of *Callichthys* and *Hoplosternum* are very lovely, but when they grow big they dig up plants or even eat small fishes. They are basically very hardy and easy to raise. *Callichthys callichthys* lives in swampy areas and muddy places so they are not sensitive to the shortage of oxygen or high temperatures. We can raise them at 25-30°C in slightly acid water. It is a good idea to create a lot of hiding places using driftwood and rock arrangements. It is known that this kind of catfish makes a foam nest like the anabantids, and that they protect their eggs under this nest. They lay from about 100 to 150 eggs. It is said that the eggs hatch within 3 to 4 days.

The porthole catfish is gentle and can live with other small fishes. It can swim very actively in the middle layer of the aquarium.

There are Many Instances of the Woodcat Spawning in Japan

Woodcats hide in the rocky caves or driftwood in the tank during the day, but when we turn off the light, they start swimming very busily in the middle layers of the aquarium. It is very easy to distinguish the sexes. The spine of the dorsal fin bends into an "S"-shape when the male matures. They hold on tightly to the female's body using their dorsal and pectoral fins during spawning activities.

They are not suitable for a community tank because they dig up the bottom sand, pull out the plants, eat small fishes, and overreact when they are frightened. However, it is easy to raise them in spite of shortages of oxygen and high temperatures.

Pimelodid Catfishes— Long Whiskers and Streamlined Body Shape

These are of the same group as the redtailed and tiger shovelnose catfishes. Most of them are peaceful and eat everything. They have especially long barbels and a streamlined body shape. Some of them are very active, but most of them are peaceful and able to live together with middle and small sized cichlids or characins.

They are very hardy and strong catfishes and there are no special methods for raising them. They are adaptable to very wide ranges of water temperature, but are sensitive to sudden changes in water quality. They like tubificid worms, bloodworms, and also flake foods. Do not catch them with your bare hands because their dorsal and pectoral fin spines are very sharp.

Glass Catfishes are the Most Suitable Community Tank Fishes

As their name indicates, the bodies of the glass catfishes appear transparent. They have a very gentle, even timid, nature. Although most of the other catfishes are of the nocturnal type, these catfishes are of the diurnal type and their active area is in the middle layers of the tank.

Plant plenty of plants. The layout of the tank should be nicely arranged with rocks and driftwood. Put this catfish in with as many of their own kind as possible because creating a group increases their activities and they will not spend most of the time hiding. They eat almost everything, including flake food, but they do not often eat food that has already fallen down to the bottom of the tank like other catfishes do.

There are Many Types of Bagrids but There are few Cases Where They have been Imported

There are many middle and small sized bagrid catfishes in Southeast Asia. However, only a few are imported into Japan. We often see species of only *Leiocassis* and *Mystus*. But in spite of the competitive prices, they are not very popular. Their nature is generally peaceful and it is possible for them to live together with similar sized fishes (black lancer catfish fight among themselves even though they are the same kind). However, when some of them grow bigger, they are likely to eat other fishes so we cannot put smaller fishes into the same tank.

The pH should be neutral, but some catfishes, for example the black lancers, the marble lanc-

ers, and the hyphen catfish, like weakly alkaline water better. Also the *Bagarius* species are fish-eaters and they are sensitive to a shortage of oxygen and to high temperatures.

Schilbeid Catfishes are Raised in Slightly Acid Old Water

The glass catfishes originating from Africa are not as transparent as the ones living in Southeast Asia. Their nature is wild compared with the peaceful nature of Southeast Asia's glass catfishes. However, generally they are gentle and spend their time in the plants with other members of the group. Their swimming ability is also a bit better than the others. It is better for them to be raised in slightly acidic old water. However, they are not very tolerant when it comes to sudden changes of their water. It is possible that they could die if they are mistreated during the water changing. You also have to be very careful of their scratches. It is important for them to be raised in a big tank with plenty of space for their swimming activities and that the water quality is kept consistent.

HOW TO RAISE
CORYDORAS CATFISHES
The Variety in the
Life-Styles of Catfishes

Corydoras are distributed all over South America. They usually swim in schools with the same kind of catfish or sometimes different kinds of catfishes. They live in a wide variety of habitats such as pellucid streams that flow very rapidly, rivers that cover many rocks, slow-running sandy areas, and among underwater plants of the main stream. The water temperature varies from close to 30°C in muddy places to below 20°C in the highland areas.

As you know, the lifestyles in these areas are quite variable, but most of these types of catfishes are very flexible. Also their nature is very gentle. It is a lot of fun to be able to raise them in an aquarium. Obviously, *Corydoras* catfishes may be raised with others of the same family; and yet they may also be raised together with tetras and small to medium-sized cichlids. Furthermore, you can enjoy collecting the various species for there are over a hundred kinds of *Corydoras*.

Points to keep in mind when buying *Corydoras* catfishes:

1. Avoid fishes immediately after they are imported (1-2 weeks) unless you have a lot of confidence.

2. Avoid fishes that have a white fleecy or slimy buildup. There is a possibility of a contagious disease that might infect the other catfishes.

3. Avoid fishes whose whiskers are disintegrating or that have lost a whisker.

4. Avoid fishes that have dim and unclear eyes as they may have been damaged or are diseased.

5. Avoid fishes that are sitting in the corner without moving. Choose an active one.

6. Avoid fishes that have hollow stomach area.

7. Avoid fishes that are breathing heavily (that have an exceptionally high number of gill movements).

8. Avoid fishes whose fins have broken rays and/or are shred in places. There is fear of it having fin rot or fungus disease. Also avoid fishes that have folded fins and any that are missing the caudal fin.

9. Avoid fishes swimming or floating awkwardly, or sometimes lying down at the bottom of the tank because they might be in an advanced stage of debility.

10. Avoid fishes that are not looking for food. It is best if we could see them in this condition by asking the shop owner to feed them.

Water Level is Not a
Major Factor in the Tank

Corydoras catfishes can be raised easily in a small aquarium. Though 30 cm of water in the tank is good enough for a few of them, 60 cm of tank water is the best. The water level (height of tank) is not very important. Most of the catfishes usually live in about 10-20 cm of water in their natural habitat. It is, therefore, better to prepare a shallow but wide aquarium. A normal size 60 cm tank will enable you to raise up to 20 of them. That is a standard.

Different Water Temperature by Species

The genus *Corydoras* is widely distributed, and the water temperatures that the various species are accustomed to are different. It is therefore better to raise the ones that like high temperatures separate from the ones that like low temperatures. The species of the low water temperature type (*barbatus, macropterus, garbei, guapore,* etc.) especially have a lack of adaptability for high temperatures and they often die when exposed to them for a long period of time. Generally, it is better to raise them at a lower temperature, at about 22-24°C, than normal for a tropical fish.

It might be necessary to change the position of an aquarium to a cooler place in the house when the temperature goes up over 30°C during the summer season.

Although *Corydoras* are basically tough and hardy fishes, they do prefer fresh, clean water. They also are big eaters, producing a great deal of excrement in proportion to their size. So, make it a rule to change a third of the water once a week. Although most tap water is fine for both the tank water and the changing water, the city water should not be used immediately after the chlorine has been neutralized, but use the water with the chlorine taken out only after it has been aerated for 3 to 4 days.

A slightly alkaline water is best for the low water temperature species, but it is not necessary to pay too much attention to it. For the general species, slightly acid water can be used by adding a little bit of peat to the filtration chamber.

Provide a Horizontal Flow of Water

There is the basic idea that the filtration should be at the bottom of the tank. It is necessary to use the filtration system at the bottom (undergravel system) to protect the catfishes from gases forming in the sand since fine sand is used for the substrate.

Also according to the number of catfishes or the layout, you can use a combination of the upper filter, floating filter, or power filter. In any case you should create a current somewhere in the tank. Especially the species that live in the rapid streams in the mountains (generally they have a long body and long nose) like the flow of water. Create a horizontal current and try to manage somehow to use a strainer with the filtration system.

Use Fine Sand for the Substrate

Corydoras often search for food by putting their heads in the sand in their native habitat, but sometimes they even sink (bury themselves) into the sand. For that reason it is better to use the fine dried sand (rounded type,

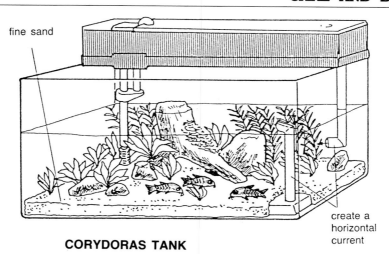

fine sand

create a
horizontal
current

CORYDORAS TANK

not angled) on the bottom of the tank.

Recently very fine sand has become available (there are many kinds and brands on the market). When you raise the catfish with regular large-grain sand they cannot go under the sand or cannot dig for food in the sand because of its coarseness. Besides their whiskers may become frayed. Place the sand in about 3 cm depth on the bottom of the tank for the *Corydoras* catfish so that they cannot uproot the plants.

Concerning the plants, it is best to use those found in the Amazon, but it is also possible to use other hardy plants such as *Microsorium, Cryptocoryne*, and *Anubias*. Put small stones firmly around the roots of the plants just to make sure the root takes hold. Distribute the plants and the small stones around the tank in an esthetically pleasing manner and create a big space in the center of the tank. Do not plant a lot of willow moss in the

tank because if it grows too thick, the *Corydoras* cannot get out easily from the bushes.

Corydoras are Big Eaters, But Try Not to Overfeed Them

Corydoras living in their natural habitats eat tiny worms and crustaceans as well as insect larvae (including mosquito larvae) that are found in the underwater plants. Under aquarium conditions you can give them tubificid worms mainly, as well as flake foods, tablet foods, and *Daphnia* for variety in the menu.

Corydoras are big eaters in spite of their body size, but there is a limited amount of food they can consume each meal. You have to pay close attention so that the quality of the water does not deteriorate because there is too much food in the tank at once. Also spread their food around the tank. The reason for this is to prevent some larger, stronger catfishes from taking all of the food.

Put the tubificid worms into a small container. Also crush the

Daphnia and give it to them to help their digestion.

Sensitivity to Chemicals

Corydoras catfishes rarely become sick. But they are very sensitive to chemicals. That is why it is essential to find their problems as soon as possible and to begin treatment earlier. If you see something strange in their activities, it is important to change the water right away. You can treat them using various commercial medications for the different diseases, but use these medications at one-half or one-third of the normal dosage. In the case of fin-rot or whisker disintegration, transfer them to a hospital tank and put a small amount of the proper commercial medication into the water.

In the case where they have a swollen stomach because of constipation, mix a small amount of laxative (for human use) with water and put it into their tank.

Should You Raise Corydoras Catfish Alone or with other Catfishes?

There is no trouble when you want to keep the same species together. It is not unusual for 2-3 species of *Corydoras* to live together in nature. When placing them together with other species, it is necessary to keep in mind that the *Corydoras* is an active catfish. As they move around all the time looking for food at the bottom of the tank, or move up all of a sudden to the water's surface for breathing, the catfish appear very nervous and cannot calm themselves down.

They will be a nuisance to the other small nocturnal catfishes. So be sure to design your tank so that each catfish can have enough room to establish its own territory in the tank.

Sometimes large fishes (for example silurid catfishes, *Polypterus* spp., cichlids) swallow a *Corydoras* catfish. In such cases, either they swallow it entirely, spit it out, or get it stuck in the mouth. In these latter cases both the *Corydoras* and the big predatory fish may die. Keeping the small fishes with fishes that have a big mouth should basically be avoided.

The Challenge of Propagation: Prepare the Aquarium for Both Hatching and Spawning

You can say one of the big attractions of owning *Corydoras* catfishes is to be able to attempt a spawning. Although there are some species that make even a professional breeder give up, many of the species are relatively easy to breed.

The list of species that spawn easily:

1. *arcuatus*-group (*ellisae*, etc.)
2. *elegans*-group (*hastatus*, etc.)
3. *Aspidoras* species.
4. *aeneus*-group (*aeneus*, *metae*, etc.)
5. *barbatus*-group (*barbatus*, *paleatus*, etc.)
6. *Brochis*-group
7. *punctatus*-group (*haraldschultzi*, etc.)

Forming a Pair: In the case of raising a few of the same species of *Corydoras*, it is important to ascertain if any pair has been formed. Sex distinctions are that a female is bigger than a male and has a greater body depth, a female's stomach area bulges out when viewed from above, a female's stomach seems to be of a pinkish color when they are carrying eggs, etc. Generally a male's body is going to be of a shiny color.

As spawning time approaches, the male tries to stick with a female, trying to get her attention, and goes around in front brushing his stomach against a female's mouth.

In the case where the Corydoras is living together with others, either move the other fish into the other tank or move only the Corydoras pair into the hatching aquarium. This is done because the eggs will be eaten by a small cichlid, a pleco, or a snail in the mixed resident aquarium if the female Corydoras spawns successfully.

There are two ways to obtain a pair. One way is to raise them from a group of young and the other one is to buy already mature fishes from a pet shop. Generally speaking, it is best to raise the Corydoras catfish from a young age because they will mature within a year. The way to choose mature fishes at the pet shop is to buy a few fish after observing them closely. But it is better to avoid buying the large catfish for they may be too old.

The Spawning Aquarium: A proper sized aquarium for spawning is about 45-60 cm (except for the long-nosed types like C. barbatus). The 90 cm tank might be too big for the pair and they may lose their passion.

Spread a thin layer of fine sand on the bottom of the tank. Because they do not always lay the eggs immediately, use a bottom filtration system in case you have to continue raising them in the breeding tank for a while. The bottom filter does not necessarily have to be the right size proportionately with the aquarium. The same bottom filter used for a 30 cm aquarium, for example, can be used for a 60 cm aquarium.

Let the water circulate slowly by providing weak aeration. Place an Amazon sword plant in a pot and loosen the willow moss; move it into the center of the aquarium. By floating something like water sprite over half the water surface you can make the pair relax. The plants are by all means necessary, but do not place them too close.

You should aim for the water temperature to be 24°C. The water is better fresh, i.e., tap water that has been aerated for about 3 days. If there is a definite pair, one female and one male Corydoras, place them in a separate tank as described before. However, if the pair is not definite, place a combination of females and males in the tank, e.g., two males with one female, two females with two males, etc..

Initially a pursuing movement can be seen before the spawning. The spawners then look for a place to spawn or they clean various spots on the glass's surface and plants in order to attach the eggs onto them. As the male lies down before before the female, the female sucks at the male's vent and retains the sperm in her mouth. The female lays 2-5 eggs at this moment and carries them, by holding the eggs with her pelvic fins, over to the spot prepared in advance. She then blows the sperm out on the eggs to fertilize them. Repeating this movement, she sticks the eggs all over the aquarium.

Most of the spawning is done in the morning or in the evening. You must not turn the light on or off all of a sudden during the actual spawning.

Artificial Incubation and Caring for the Young (Just Hatched): Although you can leave the eggs as they are, it is better to hatch them in a separate aquarium that should be prepared before tenderly transferring the eggs one by one.

As the eggs immediately after spawning are soft, remove them from the aquarium after a few minutes, when they will have had a chance to stiffen up a bit. The bottom sand is not necessary in the process of hatching in the aquarium, and it is easier to take care of them without the sand.

Gently attach the eggs to the glass, making sure to leave some space between them. But there is also a way of putting all the eggs together in a net as shown in the picture. However, although time and labor consuming, it is better to remove the eggs one by one for mold may grow on the eggs if they are removed all at once. The eggs spawned on the plants may be moved into the hatching aquarium together with the plants. Either way, a little bit of aeration is necessary.

Set the temperature to 25-26°C in the hatching tank. Then it usually takes the eggs about 3 days to hatch. Not only does it take extra time to hatch, but crippled catfish may result if the water temperature is too low. Because the hatched baby fish swim back and forth between the bottom and the surface of the water in order to breathe by using their intestines, the water level should be relatively low. Although the newly hatched fry take nutrition from their yolk, there is no problem with feeding them from the first day.

Brine shrimp are best as a beginner's food. If it is possible feed them several times a day. You can also feed them once a day, at night, if there is an ample supply of food. But, as a warning, this last procedure may be hazardous to your catfish for it may slow down the growth and the mortality rate will increase.

Three days after hatching, start feeding a paste of tubificid worms. Give the mashed tubifex after its moisture is removed by putting it on a paper filter. Powdered flake food is also good but precautions need to be taken because it makes the water dirty.

Change the water every day. Entire spawns of baby fish

sometimes happen to die because of neglect of changing the water. Use the air tubing to change the water, taking care not to suck the baby fish in. Also drain the water out and suck the bottom dirt out at the same time. Again, using the air tube, pour the same quantity of water in that was removed from the parent's aquarium. During this action, be careful with the fresh water—do not hit the baby fish directly.

RAISING *CORYDORAS*

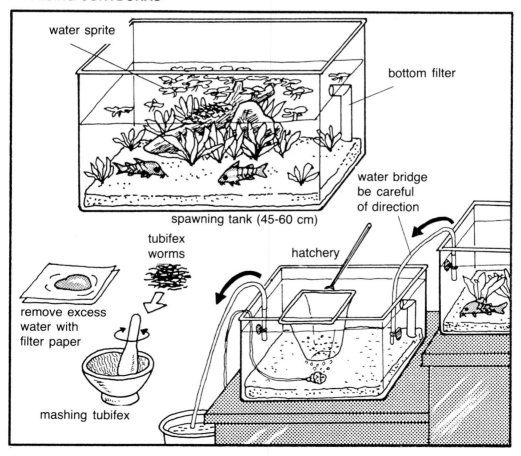

water sprite

bottom filter

spawning tank (45-60 cm)

water bridge
be careful
of direction

tubifex
worms

hatchery

remove excess
water with
filter paper

mashing tubifex

HOW TO RAISE DORADID CATFISHES
Tough But Peaceful Catfishes That Live in Quiet Waters

The doradid catfishes, except for several big ones, generally live under the vegetation near the shore or in shallow parts of lakes in quiet waters. Many small ones live in about 30 cm of water. There is plenty of food—the availability of insect larvae and mollusks near the shore is the reason why they live there. They live indifferently in sewer outlets where human waste enters, or even in swampy areas where methane gas comes up. In these types of environments, there are big differences in the water temperature and changes in the water quality around the swamp during rainy and dry seasons. This means that the doradid catfishes seem to have high adaptability to their environment and are more easily kept by humans.

Most doradids are also relatively innocuous, feeding on vegetation or small insects. People in Europe like to raise small doradids in aquaria because the doradid can live together with other small fishes and eat leftover food on the bottom of the tank.

Many people like doradid catfishes because of their resemblance to "monsters." There must be 70-80 different kinds of these catfishes, of which about 30 are imported into Japan, making them objects of collections.

Beware of Scratches and Parasites Immediately After Import

Checking the doradids when buying them is more important than raising them. It is almost impossible to import them without any scratches as they rub against each other with their sharp spines.

In many cases, they die because of fungal disease. The fungus grows on their scratches after they have been weakened from not having eaten for long stretches during importation. We can also sometimes see external parasites on the soft area around the belly. It is better to choose those catfishes with fewer scratches and those that are not thin. If possible, it is better to buy them only after you have been able to observe them carefully for about one week.

Although they are Tough Fishes, Keep the Water Clean

The pH should be neutral with the water temperature 25-27°C, although this kind of fish has a naturally strong resistance against disease. But once they get sick, it is difficult to nurse them back to health. When strong medicines or salt is administered, it is rougher on their unprotected skin than it would be on scaled fishes. Think about prevention first more than treatment and observe them daily. Sometimes their mouth gets festering red sores, the fins "melt," or the bases of the fins turn red. There are reasons for this: some of the food may have become moldy, the water may be getting old, etc. One third of the water should be changed once a week as with other tropical fishes.

It is Possible to Keep 30 Different Kinds of Doradid Together

We can say that most doradids are able to coexist together as well as being able to live together with other fishes, too. They don't kill or fight each other even if their body sizes are different. Therefore, it is possible to keep 30 different doradids in the same tank. There is nothing to worry about when raising them together when the condition of each doradid is almost the same. But it is unwise to let catfishes that differ too greatly in size swim together.

They are nocturnal fishes by nature, but we can make them actively swim out of their hiding places for observation by giving them food during the day. They eat any kind of food, like earthworms, tubificid worms, flake food, etc. You can feed them once a day, usually after putting out the light. Caution should be taken so as not to keep feeding them the same food too often. Vary their diet.

Add Plants and Driftwood

When keeping more than one doradid, you must have a particular setup because of their territoriality. There are roughly three behavioral patterns in their habitat or dwelling:

1. Some slip around and under the roots of plants.

2. Some hide and live between driftwood or rocks.

3. Some dive into the sand.

The proper layout design is necessary to satisfy all the doradids because they rest in different places at different times during the day. It is better to have a mass of plants with long roots on the surface of the water, driftwood set up complexly with rocks and tunnels on the bottom, and fine-grained river sand on the bottom. Certain layouts can be envisioned from when we frequently come across the scene in which many doradids are in one spot resting in the vicinity of the driftwood. The depth of the water doesn't matter—shallow or deep.

If it is decided that the layout should be extremely shallow, caution should be taken that the thermostat and heater be properly submerged. It is hard to control the temperature of the water if too much of the system is above the water's surface. Water currents are not especially needed. Bottom filters are good enough for filtration if the water is changed regularly. It may be better to use outside filters in combination with the bottom ones. The water can never be too clean.

By Imitating Their Natural Environment, Let's Dare Attempt Propagation Even Though There Have Been Very Few Results

Although there are very few examples of observations of doradid propagation in the aquarium, it is still possible to think about spawning them in the home aquarium (except for

DORADID AQUARIUM

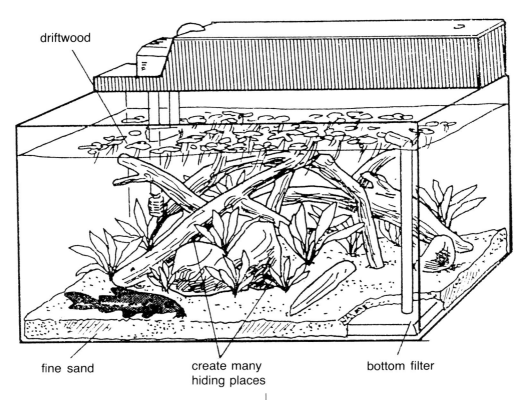

driftwood

fine sand

create many
hiding places

bottom filter

the very large species). This is probably one of the reasons why these fishes are not popular yet.

Taking a look at the whole propagation pattern of the doradids, many of them in their natural environment lay their eggs in quiet waters. There are piles of fallen leaves at the bottom of the river and they slip in and spawn under the leaves. It is said that many of them protect their eggs. Some doradids dig holes in the bottom and lay the eggs there to protect them.

Although it is difficult to reconstruct their natural environment completely, there is a possibility that they will lay and hatch eggs if the reconstruction is reasonably similar to it. It takes one year

for them to mature but their young bodies still cannot produce eggs. So you have to keep 7 to 10 of the same kind of doradid together and wait until the second year after they have been properly conditioned before you can expect results.

It is hard to sex doradid catfishes. Females have plumper bodies and they are more of a whitish color. To help condition females, try to change the weakly acid water in the beginning to alkaline or neutral water. All the fish spawn during the rainy season at once. This means we have to imitate the change in water quality by increasing the water quantity during the rainy season.

HOW TO RAISE THE LORICARIID CATFISHES
Choose the Easiest Species to Raise for Beginners

Loricariids have a long history as captive tropical fishes. They were often kept only as scavengers from the earliest times because of their subdued colors and their shapes. Many different species are imported these days that have beautiful colors and more unusual shapes, so they have become much more popular as tropical fishes.

Although there are still many uncertain points pertaining to the ecological problems in their habitat, the beautiful species of this catfish family mostly live in tributaries or small streams and they are vegetarians. There are some very important points to be aware of when raising these catfishes. In spite of the many healthy individuals, these fishes cannot survive without fresh water and plants.

You as a beginner can start by raising hardy types of catfishes like the plecos (*Hypostomus*), the sailfin plecos (*Pterygoplichthys*), or the blue-eyed pleco (*Panaque suttoni*). You can obtain the *Ancistrus* catfishes fairly easily but you need to take extra care of them because these catfishes may suddenly die when the water in their tank is being changed.

Keep Water Temperatures Lower and Avoid Extremely Acidic or Alkaline Water

The water (depending upon the habitat) should be close to pH 7.0 for the quietly colored cat-

fishes. They have a wide range in South America because they can easily adapt to their environment. But there are limits to their adaptabilities. They do not like the water if it gets too old or if it is too hard or even if there is too much alkalinity.

You should check the water quality regularly when you see the color of their body turning darker or even lighter. Because catfishes that used to live in mountain torrents crave fresh water more than other catfishes, you should make sure that their water is changed an ample amount of times. It is enough to change one half to one third of the water weekly. It is the same as changing the water for tropical fishes.

Water temperatures can vary from 20° to 27°C, but it is better to maintain the aquarium at a lower temperature to keep the oxygen from becoming depleted. When you raise these fishes in high temperature water, it is necessary to give them better air circulation by creating currents.

It is Necessary to Control the Light

The pleco catfishes like dark places in the aquarium because they are nocturnal. But it is necessary to keep lights on at times for the growing of the plants. So you should think about the design of the tank layout so that the catfishes can get enough protection or shade between the rocks or under driftwood even though the light is penetrating the water. If there is not enough space for shelter for them because there are many catfishes in the aquarium, they will fight each other to obtain and protect their shelter. That is why you should create a sufficient number of shelters for them.

The lights should be kept on for about 12 hours a day for the growing plants. If you don't see the plants growing well, either increase the wattage of the lights or leave them on for a longer period of time. You should remember that the lights are only for growing plants and that it is not a comfortable environment for the pleco catfish. Especially if you try to spawn them, leave them in the dark.

Choose Healthy Catfishes

It is very important to make the right choice when initially selecting the loricariid catfishes for your aquarium. This will decide the health and nature of the fish when it matures. It is better not to buy fishes that have been just imported because most likely they have become weakened by sudden changes in the water quality, fatigue due to long transportation, lack of food, and stress. Buy the fishes that have already gotten used to living in the quality of water in your town.

Avoid fishes that have fungus, white spot disease, or whitish eyes. Some fishes may have a hollow belly because they were not given any food during import; its even worse if their eyes have become sunken. These fish will take longer to recover and they have a much higher mortality rate than others. It is very important to choose the ones that have been fed enough food and are "fat and sassy."

You can enjoy raising the small to middle-sized loricarias and plecos even in a 60 cm aquarium. In such a tank, for example, you can raise 10 small catfishes, such as the clown pleco, ancistrus, loricarias, or farlowellas. But for larger catfishes you can raise only one or two of them in the same tank. In both cases, you have to keep watching the surface of their body and fins for scratches, spots, or other indications that something is going wrong.

Plant plenty of decorative plants and plan a nice layout using a piece of driftwood along with stones or rocks in the aquarium. You may prefer to plant water sprite for originality because the pleco catfishes like to live there. But it is difficult to grow water sprite in a tank over a long term. It is better to avoid plants that have tender leaves because the catfishes like to eat them. Use inexpensive plants such as *Vallisneria*, *Echinodorus*, etc., and a piece of driftwood, mainly using the rocks for layout.

Make Sure They are Compatible

In many cases when larger pleco catfishes are raised with other types of fishes in the same big aquarium, their dorsal fins will be picked on by large aggressive cichlids. They may also be chewed up by other, larger catfishes. It is better, therefore, not to raise them together with other

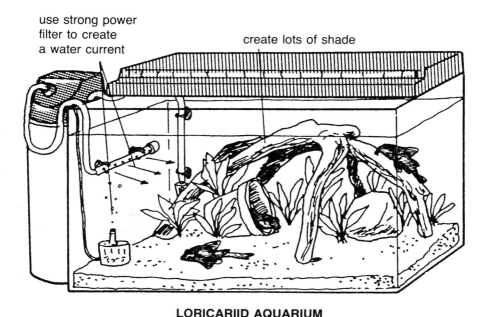

use strong power filter to create a water current

create lots of shade

LORICARIID AQUARIUM

large, aggressive fishes, such as electric catfishes, electric eels, or large size cichlids.

If you raise the pleco catfishes together with other fishes, make sure they have enough food. You had better transfer the pleco to a separate aquarium if the other types of big fishes eat all the food.

On the other hand, the pleco itself may pick on other fishes. It is possible that they could get hurt from the pleco or that they have become stressed from the pleco's nocturnal activities. For example, fishes most vulnerable to the pleco's attentions are those that have the surface of their body very wide, like the discus, or fishes that move very slowly. Small characins will also be eaten by them.

Whether they live peacefully together or not depends a lot on the abundance of food and the protection provided by their shelters.

Give Them a Variety of Foods

The main foods for the loricariid catfishes are algae and higher plants. They will die if they lack these foods. Because the function of the internal organs is designed primarily for herbivores, if they consume only proteins or fats they put more pressure on their digestive system and the chances of them breeding diminish. This means that they do not really need animal fat.

You may feed them artificial foods designed for carp and vegetable flake food in addition to live tubificid worms and *Daph-*

nia. It is said that they are fed boiled oatmeal, spinach, lettuce, and celery in the United States.

But the best of all is natural vegetation. It is a good idea to strengthen or increase the light. Long hours of illumination will make moss and algae grow on the sides of the glass and the plants. You can also put aluminum foil around the aquarium and maximize the use of the fluorescent light. There is also another way. Place a small separate tank containing stones and pieces of driftwood under direct sunlight to grow algae and plants naturally. Transfer these plants to the original aquarium from time to time once they have grown sufficiently or even transfer the catfishes to the algae aquarium (if the water quality and temperature are comparable).

METHODS FOR KEEPING *SYNODONTIS*
Determine the Aquarium Size to Fulfill Your Enjoyment

Synodontis species form the largest group of catfishes in Africa. From this group come the most popular aquarium fishes because of their beautiful patterns. Many things must be considered during their care and feeding.

For example, fully grown fishes can be from 15 cm to over 50 cm in length. Also the *Synodontis* originating from the basin of the Zaire (Congo) River live in an entirely different environment than the *Synodontis* that live in the waters of Lakes Victoria, Malawi, and other Rift Lakes. Therefore, it is necessary to choose the species and the aquarium size carefully after deciding your pleasure. If you decide on a mixed species tank, African or other types, you must be sure that they can live together harmoniously and do not grow too large.

The following species, *S. schal*, *S. notatus*, and *S. acanthomias*, are carnivorous and should not be mixed with other small species. A broad mixture of *Synodontis* species requires a 120 cm aquarium. If you want to enjoy watching a single species grow to its full maturity, a 60 cm aquarium will be sufficient for a medium-sized fish. Finally, each species presents its own challenge when the object is its propagation. An aquarium for this purpose should be at least 90 cm.

There is a Large Difference in the Quality of the Water for Each Habitat of the Group

The majority of African riverine *Synodontis* species gravitate to neutral, soft, and slightly acid waters. It isn't necessary to be too concerned about water quality for these species. However, *Synodontis* are extremely susceptible to stagnant and nitrogen-rich water such as water containing ammonia. Such water could be a major factor in producing sickly fishes. *Synodontis* species from Lakes Tanganyika and Malawi prefer water with a high alkali content. The most well known species from that type of environment are *S. multipunctatus*, *S. dhonti*, *S. eurystomus*, *S. victoria*, and *S. njassae*. Dolomite or coral sand will produce hard, alkaline water. However, chemicals can be purchased that will produce the same conditions. If the quality of water for the above-mentioned *Synodontis* is not suitable they will turn black in color and become sick. Basically, it is important for freshwater fishes that you change one third of the water content of their tank once a week. If the fish turn dark extra care must be exercised. If the water becomes stagnant, their eyes develop a white film, their fins close, and their swimming becomes sluggish. Additionally, the body loses its shine and turns a whitish color, the area around the mouth turns red, it loses its whiskers, and it swims with its nose tilted up. Consequently,

(Right) *Synodontis brichardi*. Photo by Hans Joachim Richter.

(Below) *Synodontis flavitaeniatus*. Photo by Burkhard Kahl.

changing the water becomes imperative. The water temperature should be approximately 24°C. In their native habitat water temperature ranges from 20° to 28°C. Adaptable as they are to changes in temperature, extreme changes should be avoided. Young fish require water temperatures of 26°C to avoid white-spot disease. As they mature the temperature should be gradually decreased.

The Diet Should Be Varied

Synodontis like vegetation and a slow current such as are found in lakes, ponds, and river basins. The majority of the species are nocturnal. They begin actively searching for food at evening time. Although primarily vegetarians they will eat larval insects both from the surface and off the bottom. Small teeth enable them to scrape algae from rocks and sunken trees and feed on grassy vegetation. Continuous feeding of a single item is not advisable as they have a broad taste in food. The digestive system of *Synodontis* is very compatible with vegetable matter. Therefore, it is advisable to create a climate in the aquarium for the growth of algae. A separate tank with rocks and driftwood can be used to grow algae that can then be transferred to the catfish aquarium. These rocks and driftwood should be changed every two or three days. Besides algae, boiled spinach is considered a good food. Basically, moss and algae are suitable and carp pellets can be substituted. Other than these

(like ordinary fishes), flake foods, tubifex worms, bloodworms (chironomids), krill, nymphs, shrimp, and crickets are acceptable foods. Feeding should be twice daily, morning and evening. Some species develop slightly different tastes as they mature. *S. petricola* when young prefers a diet of young aquatic insects. The important point in feeding is to discover the particular needs of the fish.

The Aquarium Should Contain Many Hiding Places

This is a characteristic need of *Synodontis*, especially in a community environment. Both small and large fishes will eat tender plants that are planted in the aquarium. Therefore, plants for esthetic reasons become an exercise in futility. In their native environment they seem to live in thick growths of *Vallisneria*. Plenty of aeration and water movement must also be provided. Small species can be used when mixing a variety of *Synodontis* in the same aquarium, such as *S. alberti, S. flavitaeniatus, S. contractus, S. nigriventris, S. multipunctatus, S. brichardi,* and *Mochokiella paynei*. Large species, such as *S. acanthomias, S. notatus, S. schal, S. nigrita, S. nigromaculata* and *S. angelicus*, being rather predacious, are not suitable for a community aquarium. However, if you wish to try setting up a community aquarium it is best to have about 10 fish with many hiding places in a complicated layout. Only *S. angelicus* seldom fights with other fishes.

Synodontis are More Tolerant of Medication than Many Other Types of Catfishes

Do not be too concerned about abrasions that happen during the shipment of Synodontis. They are fairly sturdy fishes and are curable by the medications that are commonly used for abrasions. It is best to maintain a high water temperature when they are small because they often contract white-spot disease. It can be cured with commercial medications if it is detected in the early stages. But an illness that appears to have all the symptoms of white-spot disease, but with the spots becoming larger and turning yellow in color, needs to be well cared for. The treatment for this illness is very difficult and there is a very high mortality rate. The illness is very contagious. During the treatment the water temperature should be higher than that required for white-spot illness and the dosage of the medication should be increased. Stagnant water will retard the recovery rate.

Propagation is Not Easy, But It is Rewarding

The successful ratio of propagation with Synodontis species is extremely low, especially for two of the species, *S. nigriventris* and *S. multipunctatus*. They spawn but the parents do not show any interest in the large quantity of eggs produced. Synodontis raised commercially in hatcheries in eastern and southern Asia are fed hormones for increased propagation, but this method is not recommended for individual aquaria.

The true reward for the aquarist results from creating a natural environment that induces natural propagation. If unsuccessful, you are probably only lacking in numbers of fish. It is very difficult for only two fish to spawn. The important points for propagation are as follows:

1) At least 10 or more fish must be in the community.

2) A large aquarium with complicated layouts and hideouts to avoid domination or fighting among the group is needed.

SYNODONTID AQUARIUM

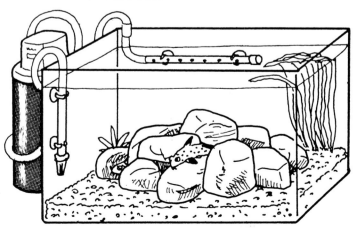

Synodontis require lots of room and open spaces. They are basically nocturnal and prefer hiding during the day, so create hiding places, too.

Arius seemani. Photo by Burkhard Kahl.

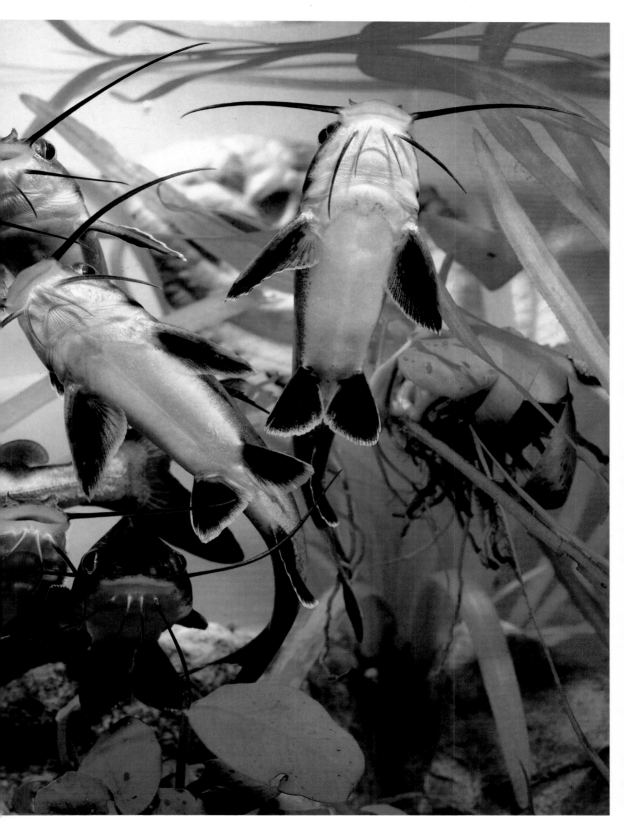

3) Choose small fishes, larger sized fishes require a numerically larger grouping and of course a larger tank.

4) Immature fish will not spawn; allow two to three years from time of import before beginning propagation attempts.

5) Once they have matured, since spawning usually occurs during the rainy season, you can stimulate the fish by changing the pH, such as suddenly replacing old water with fresh water.

6) Their diet should not consist of a single item—the types of food offered should be varied.

7) Some species have special spawning requirements that must be accommodated. For example, *S. multipunctatus* must be mixed with African mouth-brooding cichlids.

The sex of the *Synodontis* can be determined by the following criteria. Generally, males are smaller than females. As the male nears maturity a small projection can be observed at the front of its anal fin.

Although females have a similar projection it is rounded, smaller, and symmetrical. The color of the male is darker and their face is more sharply defined.

Looking at a profile of the female (viewed top to bottom) their stomachs are fuller than those of the males.

Plastic tubes or pipes make ideal hiding places for *Synodontis* and other nocturnal fishes.

Wood covered with algae makes excellent cover and food for *Synodontis* and other catfish,too. The wood can be kept outside in a sunlight aquarium and moved into the catfish tank when it has a rich covering of algae.

Imaginative rock formations which produce caves are loved by *Synodontis*.

CARE AND FEEDING METHODS OF
MALAPTERURUS ELECTRICUS
Use the Top Filter
Because of Digging in the Sand

Electric catfish are well known for their unique mode of life. They are not known for their beauty but rather for their odd appearance. They grow to be about one meter long in their native habitat and over 30 cm in an aquarium. For this reason the size of the tank should be at least 60 cm or longer. They are easily adaptable to the quality and temperature of the water, however the most suitable water should be of neutral to weak acidity and the temperature about 25°C. They are nocturnal, somewhat lazy and inactive, yet they build barricades by digging sand in the bottom or turning around small objects such as driftwood. This action causes the bottom filter to function improperly. It is recommended that only the top filter be used.

The fish will also pull out or bite off aquarium plants, causing problems with a bottom filter. The aquarium should have a firmly weighted lid on top.

For Safety,
Remove the Fishes When
Changing the Aquarium Water

The layout of the aquarium is extremely difficult for the reasons just mentioned. It is necessary to secure the driftwood pieces to a flat base that then can be weighted with rocks to keep it in place. The discharge of electricity by electric catfish lasts only a thousandth of a second and the current is small, but its voltage reaches between 400 and 500 volts. (Electric eels can produce as much as 800 volts.) You can receive a significant amount of electric shock when reaching into the tank; fish only 10 cm in length can generate over 100 volts. Therefore, remove the fish when changing the water in the tank. A large net should be used (they very sel-

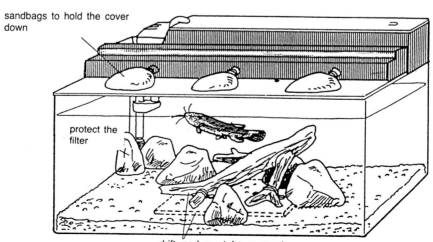

sandbags to hold the cover down

protect the filter

driftwood must be secured to heavy plate under the gravel

(Above) *Chaca bankanensis*. Photo by Hans Joachim Richter. (Facing page) *Pseudacanthicus spinosus*. Photo by Burkhard Kahl.

dom become violent). Then place them in a separate aquarium or plastic bucket filled with the new water. (Make sure the handle of the net is not wet.)

**Do Not Keep
With Other Fishes,
Even of the Same Species**

Cohabitation is impossible because of the voltage discharge. The other fish may not be killed by the electrical discharge, but they become very stressed and affected every time electricity is discharged, evidenced by a strong territorial awareness and a tendency to fight fiercely among their own kind. Only in their natural environment will they form into large groups at shoals for the laying and fertilization of eggs.

Feeding should be done individually. Foods for young fish are tubificid worms, bloodworms (chironomids), and killifishes. As they mature, change the food to goldfish and gradually to artificial food and fish meat. They are voracious eaters and will become obese if the feeding is not controlled.

Excretion will cause a high concentration of nitrates in the water, which in turn causes a loss of appetite and a whitish color on their eyes and body. Be sure to remove leftover food and change the water regularly.

KEEPING *OTOCINCLUS*

A Diamond in the Rough

Because they are inexpensive and easily replaced, not much attention has been given to the care of *Otocinclus* species. Lately, however, many strikingly beautiful types have been imported and have become extremely popular. You will notice a beautiful body sheen and development to maturity with unimaginable beauty even though in an aquarium. Feeding must be varied. In nature, *Otocinclus*, like plecos, enjoy quiet circulation, a shallow pond, relatively low water temperatures, and basins of any stream. They will survive in many different environments.

Create Atmosphere with Plants

Otocinclus inhabit the Paraguay River and its tributaries where the currents are fairly strong. They live around the roots of water sprite and reach 40 to 50 mm in length. It is very rare to find them in any other places. Knowing these circumstances you should have quantities of floating plants. Water sprite requires very strong light. Water wisteria is a substitute. The pH should be around 7.0. The water temperature should be between 25° and 28°C. Strong water circulation is recommended. Feed them bloodworms and tubifex worms and from time to time flake food in order to maintain a good diet. Keep in mind they are voracious eaters so provide for them accordingly. Do not allow the water to become stagnant. *O. arnoldi* are most plentiful in their native habitat and therefore are easily obtainable.

They are quite adaptable as they live in the main stream and tributaries as well as swamps. This species likes the vegetation

OTOCINCLUS AQUARIUM

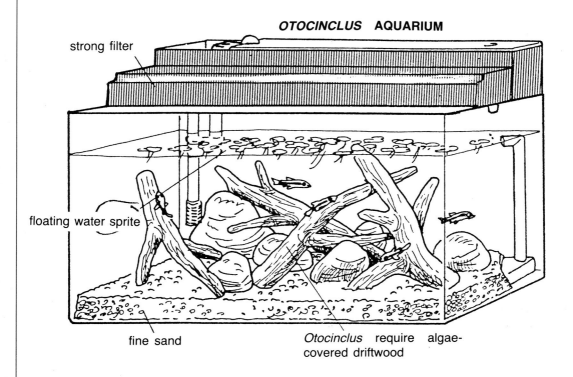

strong filter

floating water sprite

fine sand

Otocinclus require algae-covered driftwood

growing around and underneath fallen trees. They become undernourished and die if not fed enough vegetable matter.

If there is a limitation on the amount of natural vegetation you can provide, you may substitute carp food, vegetable flake food, and boiled spinach. Although they will eat tubificid worms, they are not the most suitable. Water quality must be carefully observed.

The large quantities of *Otocinclus* recently imported from clear waters need lower water temperatures, i.e., 20° to 23°C. The water should be shallow, and gravel and some larger stones should be placed on the bottom. Good water circulation is necessary.

This fish may die suddenly in highly concentrated nitrogen compounds (ammonia, nitrites, nitrates) which may be caused by too many fish in the same aquarium. If possible, feeding should take place in a quiet and spacious aquarium. For a community aquarium small characins are the best choice for cohabitation. Second or third choices would be *Corydoras* or *Microgeophagus*, which are from the same area.

(Facing page) A male *Rineloricara castroi* guarding his eggs which are just about to hatch.(Above) A closeup of the eggs. Two have already died and the male sucked out their contents to prevent fungus growth! (Below) A closeup of the eggs immediately before hatching. Series of photos by Hans Joachim Richter.

METHODS FOR THE KEEPING OF JAPANESE CATFISHES

When Collecting Fishes be Careful of Abrasion and a Lack of Oxygen

Local collecting of Japanese catfishes, such as the bagrid catfish *Pseudobagrus aurantiacus*, is possible.

Larger fishes can be caught with a fishing pole but the use of a hook and its inevitable damage to the mouth will make feeding impossible.

For collecting the smaller species a four-cornered net can be used. Put each fish into an individual bag for carrying home to avoid damaging their fins and tails.

In transport, an air pump or oxygen tank will be needed as they become very weak when not provided with sufficient oxygen. Initially put one-third of the required amount of medication for abrasions into the aquarium before stocking it with the fishes. Since catfish have no scales they will be adversely affected by excessive medication.

Avoid Rising Water Temperatures in the Summer Season

The size of the aquarium should be more than 60 cm as these fishes are rigidly territorial. When mixing many fish of the same species an abundance of hideouts will avoid the destruction of the weaker fish during the night. The species of bagrids (for ex. *Pseudobagrus aurantiacus*) will often dominate other fishes. You may use either top or bottom filters as long as filtration is sufficient. Once the catfishes have become accustomed to the aquarium environmentally they are hardy and easy to feed. However, the water must be partially changed regularly to maintain water quality. Although Japanese catfishes do not need a heating system, maintaining the water temperature at around 20°C will eliminate any differences in the water during winter months and the rainy season. This precaution will avoid white-spot disease. Do not allow excessive increases in water temperatures. Keep your

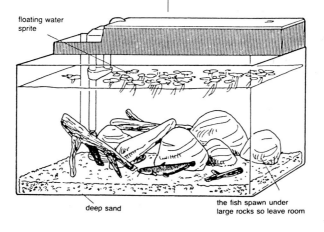

floating water sprite

deep sand

the fish spawn under large rocks so leave room

aquarium in a cool place. *Leiobagrus reini*, for instance, are not adaptable to higher water temperatures.

Simulate River Beds in Your Aquarium

Create a river layout without river mud. For *Leiobagrus reini* use river sand with small-sized gravel. Since spawning occurs under the bottom rocks, provide pieces of broken flower pots or similar sized stones to make the fish feel at home. These can easily be provided.Japanese catfishes spawn among water plants close to the river banks during the months of May and June. Foods recommended for *Leiobagrus reini* are krill, frozen mysis, small shrimp, and blood-worms. Additional foods for larger catfishes are killifishes and other small fishes, but be sure to keep the water clean.

METHOD FOR KEEPING *CHACA BANKANENSIS*
The Water Must be Slightly Acid and Quiet

This fish has enjoyed many years of popularity due to its ostentatious name, a very broad mouth, and a cute face with small eyes the size of sesame seeds. Being nocturnal they lie without movement on the bottom of the tank during daylight hours. It is difficult to determine whether they are dead or alive until a small fish swims in front of them. Any such fish will be devoured in a split second.

The water temperature should be around 26° or 28°C (as they become accustomed to the environment the temperature should be lowered), and it should be slightly acid and quiet. Avoid sudden changes of water, as they do not like new or clear

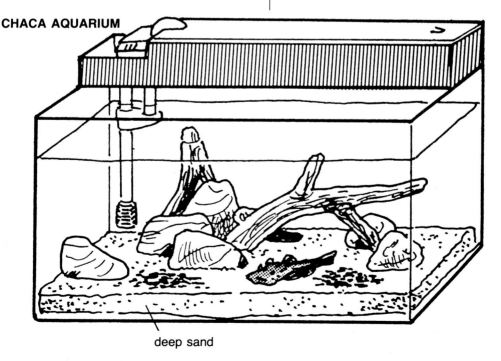

CHACA AQUARIUM

deep sand

A pair of *Corydoras aeneus*. The female is sucking sperm from the male in the characteristic T position. In the photo below, typical *Corydoras* eggs as they are hatching. The eggs are clear when laid and get darker as they come closer to hatching. On the facing page, the female first spits some sperm, then presses the eggs against the sperm on a glass plate. She carries the eggs in her clasped ventral fins. Series photos by Hans Joachim Richter.

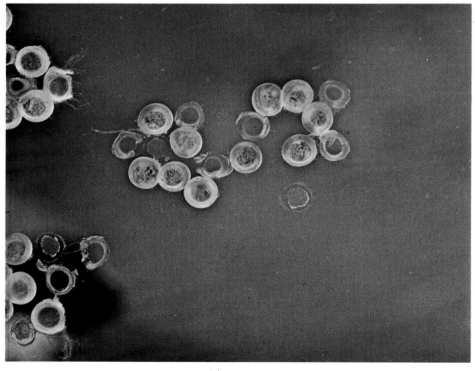

178

water. The aquarium layout should be simple, with rocks and plants, and hideouts should be scattered and camouflaged by driftwood and peat. They are carnivorous and not suitable for a community aquarium. What they can put in their mouth they will eat. They will not feel comfortable with other species who live on the bottom, kick up sand, and swim vigorously.

METHOD FOR KEEPING CANDIRU
Mixing These Species With Large Fishes can Produce Adverse Results

The majority of candiru inhabit areas with a good current, providing a flow of water and plenty of oxygen.

They enjoy water temperatures of around 22° to 23°C but you must be careful to observe whether or not these temperatures produce white-spot disease.

The species from higher altitudes of Peru, Bolivia, and southern Brazil prefer low water temperatures.

The most important concern is to determine if the species are suitable for cohabitation. Generally candiru are not nervous and are quite tame, but avoid mixing them with less active fishes that are smaller in size. The mixture of active candiru with larger fishes usually results in their becoming feed for the larger fishes.

When attempting to attack large fishes candiru will form a large group but only if the intended victim is old or weak. This does not seem to be any problem in a community aquarium. The layout should consist of rocks and small-sized gravel instead of sand. This will prevent cloudiness. Care must be taken that small fishes are not sucked into the intake of the filter. A very simple water drop-in system can be used. Change one third of the water once a week.

CANDIRU AQUARIUM

special filters which will prevent the candiru from being sucked in

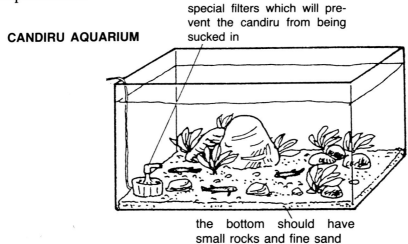

the bottom should have small rocks and fine sand

THE PROPAGATION
OF CATFISHES
Corydoras

Once a mating pair of this species is formed, move them into a spawning tank with the water temperature at 23° to 25°C. (Besides the pair put one or two additional males in the spawning tank.) The male chasing a female stimulates her with his mouth to induce spawning. The female inhales (or sucks) from the lower part of the males body for 20-30 seconds. During that time they are absolutely motionless. They then part and the female tilts her head down quietly for several seconds. The female receives the male sperm in her mouth and then lays several eggs 2mm in diameter. At this stage the fertilized eggs are kept in the female's pelvic fin basket. Once the female starts to swim again, she attaches the eggs where there is water current, on plants or on the surface of the glass. The eggs hatch in 2-3 days; the young can be fed small brine shrimp and ground tubifex worms.

Royal Farlowella, Sturisoma aureum

Place a thin layer of gravel in the spawning tank. Use the upper filter for filtration and provide a good water current. Extra aeration should be provided. The water temperature should be around 27°C. Bedding for spawning should be concentrated around driftwood. Provide a well balanced diet for the parents by feeding them mainly vegetarian flake food and tubifi-cid worms. Spawning takes place in the aquarium on the glass surface and driftwood where water currents exist. Eggs are yellow in color and protected by the male. It takes about one week for incubation. Baby fish grow naturally by eating organic compounds, but they may be given flake food. One third or one quarter of the water should be changed once a week. Baby fish must be raised in fresh water. Be sure to grow algae in a separate tank as the fish start feeding on it about a week after hatching. Boiled spinach, although usable, can cause cloudiness in the water. They start eating tubificid worms in 3-4 months.

A closeup of a male *Sturisoma* guarding his eggs. Photo by R. G. Lawrence.

The male *Sturisoma panamense* guarding his eggs. These were spawned on a leaf in a dark part of the aquarium since no cave was available. Photo by R. G. Lawrence.

Young *Sturisoma* a few weeks after hatching. Photo by R. G. Lawrence.

Measurement Conversion Factors

When you know—	Multiply by—	To find—
Length:		
Millimeters (mm)	0.04	inches (in)
Centimeters (cm)	0.4	inches (in)
Meters (m)	3.3	feet (ft)
Meters (m)	1.1	yards (yd)
Kilometers (km)	0.6	miles (mi)
Inches (in)	2.54	centimeters (cm)
Feet (ft)	30	centimeters (cm)
Yards (yd)	0.9	meters (m)
Miles (mi)	1.6	kilometers (km)
Area:		
Square centimeters (cm^2)	0.16	square inches (sq in)
Square meters (m^2)	1.2	square yards (sq yd)
Square kilometers (km^2)	0.4	square miles (sq mi)
Hectares (ha)	2.5	acres
Square inches (sq in)	6.5	square centimeters (cm^2)
Square feet (sq ft)	0.09	square meters (m^2)
Square yards (sq yd)	0.8	square meters (m^2)
Square miles (sq mi)	1.2	square kilometers (km^2)
Acres	0.4	hectares (ha)
Mass (Weight):		
Grams (g)	0.035	ounces (oz)
Kilograms (kg)	2.2	pounds (lb)
Ounces (oz)	28	grams (g)
Pounds (lb)	0.45	kilograms (kg)
Volume:		
Milliliters (ml)	0.03	fluid ounces (fl oz)
Liters (L)	2.1	pints (pt)
Liters (L)	1.06	quarts (qt)
Liters (L)	0.26	U.S. gallons (gal)
Liters (L)	0.22	Imperial gallons (gal)
Cubic centimeters (cc)	16.387	cubic inches (cu in)
Cubic meters (cm^3)	35	cubic feet (cu ft)
Cubic meters (cm^3)	1.3	cubic yards (cu yd)
Teaspoons (tsp)	5	millimeters (ml)
Tablespoons (tbsp)	15	millimeters (ml)
Fluid ounces (fl oz)	30	millimeters (ml)
Cups (c)	0.24	liters (L)
Pints (pt)	0.47	liters (L)
Quarts (qt)	0.95	liters (L)
U.S. gallons (gal)	3.8	liters (L)
U.S. gallons (gal)	231	cubic inches (cu in)
Imperial gallons (gal)	4.5	liters (L)
Imperial gallons (gal)	277.42	cubic inches (cu in)
Cubic inches (cu in)	0.061	cubic centimeters (cc)
Cubic feet (cu ft)	0.028	cubic meters (m^3)
Cubic yards (cu yd)	0.76	cubic meters (m^3)
Temperature:		
Celsius (°C)	multiply by 1.8, add 32	Fahrenheit (°F)
Fahrenheit (°F)	subtract 32, multiply by 0.555	Celsius (°C)

BIBLIOGRAPHY

Berg, L.S. 1947. *Classification of Fishes Both Recent and Fossil.* J. W. Edwards, Ann Arbor, Michigan. 517pp.

Burgess, W. E. 1989. *An Atlas of Freshwater and Marine Catfishes—A Preliminary Survey of the Siluriformes.* T.F.H. Publications, Inc. Neptune City, New Jersey. 782pp.

Chardon, M. 1968. Anatomie compare de l'appareil de Weber et des structure connexes chez les Siluriformes. *Ann. Mus. Roy. Afr. Centr., ser. 8, Sci. Zool., #69,* 277pp.

Fink, S. V. & W. L. Fink, 1981. Interrelationships of the ostariophysan fishes (Teleostei). *J. Linn Soc. (Zool.),* 72(4): 297-353.

Greenwood, P. H., D. E. Rosen, S. H. Weitzman, & G. S. Myers, 1966. Phyletic studies of Teleostean fishes, with a provisional classification of living forms. *Bull. Amer. Mus. Nat. Hist.,* 131(4):339-456.

Lundberg, J. G. & J. N. Baskin, 1969. The caudal skeleton of the catfishes, order Siluriformes. *Amer. Mus. Novitates,* #398, 49pp.

Novacek, M. J. & L. G. Marshall, 1976. Early biogeographic history of ostariophysan fishes. *Copeia,* 1976(1): 1-12.

Regan, C. T. 1911. The classification of the teleostean fishes of the order Ostariophysi. 2. Siluroidea. *Ann. Mag. Nat. Hist.,* ser. 8, 8: 553-577.

Roberts, T. R., 1972. Ecology of fishes in the Amazon and Congo basins. *Bull. Mus. Comp. Zool., Harvard.* 143(2): 117-147.

Rineloricaria microlepidogaster sitting on his eggs. Note the round, bushy-face of the male. The spawning site was a hollow bamboo tube. Photo by R. Zukal.

The bamboo tube with the top removed. The male guards and tends the eggs. The female stays in close proximity to the nesting site. This is not a difficult group to spawn. Photo by R. Zukal.

INDEX

INDEX

INDEX